Exploring Talk in Schools

Exploring Talk in Schools

Inspired by the Work of Douglas Barnes

edited by

Neil Mercer

and

Steve Hodgkinson

Los Angeles • London • New Delhi • Singapore • Washington DC

KH

First published 2008

SAGE Publications Ltd
1 Oliver's Yard
55 City Road
London EC1Y 1SP

SAGE Publications Inc.
2455 Teller Road
Thousand Oaks, California 91320

SAGE Publications India Pvt Ltd
B 1/I 1 Mohan Cooperative Industrial Area
Mathura Road
New Delhi 110 044

SAGE Publications Asia-Pacific Pte Ltd
33 Pekin Street #02-01
Far East Square
Singapore 048763

Library of Congress Control Number 2008923545

British Library Cataloguing in Publication data

A catalogue record for this book is available from the British Library

ISBN 978-1-84787-378-1
ISBN 978-1-84787-379-8 (pbk)

Typeset by C&M Digitals (P) Ltd., Chennai, India
Printed in Great Britain by T. J. International Ltd, Padstow, Cornwall
Printed on paper from sustainable resources

10/5/09

Contents

Contributors

Robin Alexander
Fellow of Wolfson College, University of Cambridge
Professor of Education Emeritus, University of Warwick
Director of the Primary Review
Faculty of Education
University of Cambridge
United Kingdom

Tamara Ball
Ph.D. Candidate, Education Department
Faculty of Social Sciences
University of California at Santa Cruz
United States of America

Douglas Barnes
Former Reader in Education
School of Education
University of Leeds
United Kingdom

Laura Black
Lecturer in Literacy
School of Education
University of Manchester
United Kingdom

Maria Lucia Castanheira
Faculdade de Educação
Universidade Federal de Minas Gerais
Brazil

Courtney B Cazden
Charles William Eliot Professor of Education, Emerita
Harvard Graduate School of Education
Harvard University
United States of America

Lyn Dawes
Senior Lecturer in Education
School of Education
University of Northampton
United Kingdom

Carol Gilles
Associate Professor of Reading and Language Arts
College of Education
University of Missouri-Columbia
United States of America

Judith Green
Professor of Education
Gevirtz School of Education
University of California at Santa Barbara
United States of America

Frank Hardman
Professor in Educational Studies
Centre for Language Learning Research
School of Education Studies
University of York
United Kingdom

Steve Hodgkinson
Research Fellow
Department of Psychiatry and Psychotherapy
University Hospital Ulm
Germany

Neil Mercer
Professor of Education & Fellow of Hughes Hall
Faculty of Education
University of Cambridge
United Kingdom

Kathryn Mitchell Pierce
Writing Instructional Support Specialist
Wydown Middle School
Clayton, Missouri
United States of America

Phil Scott
Professor of Science Education
School of Education
University of Leeds
United Kingdom

Yvette Solomon
Reader
Department of Educational Research
Lancaster University
United Kingdom

Gordon Wells
Professor of Education
Faculty of Social Sciences
University of California at Santa Cruz
United States of America

Beth Yeager
Director, Center for Education Research
Gevirtz Graduate School of Education
University of California at Santa Barbara
United States of America

Introduction

Steve Hodgkinson and Neil Mercer

One could be forgiven for thinking that the single greatest challenge facing children as they grow up in the twenty-first century is how they can become productive members of an increasingly technological society. Certainly many school curricula reflect the importance placed on children understanding the application of innovation, technology and their interconnectedness in our global society. That said, we perhaps take too much for granted a more fundamental aspect of the human condition: our use of language, principally speech, to communicate with each other. This is particularly important in the formative years of our development, including the many years we spend as children in school.

Classroom talk, by which children make sense of what their peers and teachers mean, has been the subject of school-based educational research for more than forty years now. In that time, its significance has been redefined as individualistic, cognitive theories of learning gave way to more social, culturally located interpretations of learning. It is now appreciated that classroom talk is not merely a conduit for the sharing of information, or a means for controlling the exuberance of youth; it is the most important educational tool for guiding the development of understanding and for jointly constructing knowledge. As the chapters in this book will make clear, research has provided a wealth of good reasons why policy makers and teachers should give more attention to improving the quality of classroom talk.

More than thirty years ago, when this field of research was still in its infancy, Douglas Barnes wrote 'From Communication to Curriculum', a succinct account of the kinds of classroom talk he observed in a Leeds secondary school. He noted that often the odds were stacked against pupils being able to use talk productively in the classroom, because of the rigid and formalised way teachers required children to engage in dialogue. Since then, the book has become a core text for the more enlightened initial teacher education courses, and the clear but profound message that it conveyed has reverberated across time.

Today, the relevance of the ideas expressed in it is an enduring legacy of the work of Douglas Barnes, and a source of inspiration for the many educationalists who have adopted his ideas in their own work.

In this book, we have gathered together some of those leading educationalists who have been inspired by Douglas's work, and asked them to write about their own work on classroom talk. In doing so, we have been conscious of the need to bridge what often seems like a vast conceptual gulf between practitioners and researchers – a gulf that Douglas bridged so well. Hence, each of the contributions locates the research firmly within the practice of classroom teaching, and outlines practical steps that may be taken to develop effective classroom interaction in many different contexts.

In the opening chapter, 'Exploratory Talk for Learning', Douglas Barnes summarises something of what he has learnt from his years as a schoolteacher and as a researcher about how pupils learn in school and how teachers can best help them. During his time at the University of Leeds he set out to investigate what role spoken and written language can, at best, play in young people's learning in school. Later on, he came to define the relationship between teachers and learners less in terms of language and more as the kinds of access to the processes of learning that teachers made possible. The communication system that a teacher sets up in a lesson shapes the roles that pupils can play, and goes some distance in determining the kinds of learning that they engage in. Thus he deals not only with pupils' learning, but also with what teachers do to influence this, while at the same time acknowledging that a teacher's attention is not given solely to the content of what is being taught; it is also necessary to manage social relations in the classroom, and failure in this latter respect will endanger any progress in learning. The management of these two responsibilities – which at times can seem almost to be in conflict – is central to the skill of teaching.

As a very practical example of how 'guided' talk can enhance pupils' understanding of new ideas, Phil Scott's chapter, 'Talking a Way to Understanding in Science Classrooms', focuses on the talk of the science classroom and in particular on the ways in which teachers can interact with pupils, in whole-class settings, to support the meaningful learning of scientific concepts. The kind of scenario developed here concerns how a teacher might support a class of pupils, over a period of time, in moving from an initial everyday understanding of a specific phenomenon (such as an object falling) to a scientific explanation of that same phenomenon (perhaps in terms of gravity). How might we characterise the kinds of talk used as a teacher interacts with pupils during a series of lessons and different teaching purposes are addressed? The approach Scott takes on these issues draws upon socio-cultural theory and recent studies of meaning making in classroom settings (including those he has carried out with Eduardo Mortimer). Particular attention is paid to the demands upon teachers as they act 'in the gap' between pupil understandings and scientific views and to the sophisticated level of insight which is required of teachers if productive dialogue is to flourish in classrooms. Set out in these broad terms, this chapter returns to precisely the same kinds of issues which Douglas Barnes addressed so perceptively and elegantly over thirty-five years ago in his own analyses of the ways in which language underpins the teaching and learning of science.

In their chapter, 'From Exploratory Talk to Critical Conversations', Kathryn M. Pierce and Carol Gilles draw on their observations of how pupils in the USA use classroom talk to generate and think through their ideas in elementary and middle school classrooms. Their work with literature discussion groups over the past twenty years has allowed them to listen closely to the ways students talk about the books they have read. They see talk as providing a window into students' thinking as they work at understanding and generating new understanding. Using Barnes's idea of 'exploratory talk' has helped them to appreciate how students use language to gain new, collaborative insights. Students draw on books and each other's contributions to begin to critique contemporary society, generating a sense of hope that things can change and inspiring one another to take thoughtful, new action. In their efforts to 'unpack' exploratory talk, to figure out what students can do with this talk and what different forms it takes, Pierce and Gilles have begun to look at what they call *critical conversations*. Critical conversations involve students engaged in exploratory talk that includes questioning or challenging beliefs. Pierce and Gilles suggest that these conversations can only take place within a supportive learning community in which learners feel comfortable taking risks, putting forth tentative ideas, and raising difficult questions that examine their own and others' beliefs and actions.

Moving across several time zones, but on a similar theme, in the next chapter, 'The Value of Exploratory Talk', Neil Mercer and Lyn Dawes describe how a programme of classroom-based research inspired by Barnes's work has found that group discussion can contribute not only to the development of children's language and reasoning skills, but also to their individual, curriculum-related learning. Building upon Barnes's work showing how group discussions in the classroom enable children to explore ideas, try out new ways of thinking and solve problems together, Mercer and Dawes develop further the concept of exploratory talk, showing how it can be used to shape both communications between teachers and pupils and talk amongst pupils. The findings of their research have direct implications for how teachers should interact with their students, for how they should prepare students for working effectively together, and for what students themselves should understand about their use of language as a tool for reasoning and learning. Links are made with the concept of 'dialogic teaching', as described by Alexander (Chapter 6), with Scott's work on talk in science education (Chapter 2) and with Solomon and Black's work on mathematics education (Chapter 5). The research Mercer and Dawes describe has generated a practical approach to teaching called *Thinking Together*, which has now been used successfully by many teachers in the UK and in other parts of the world, and its essential features are set out in their chapter.

'Talking to Learn and Learning to Talk in the Mathematics Classroom' is an account of the research undertaken by Yvette Solomon and Laura Black on one of the most distinctive and yet perhaps under-emphasised elements of Douglas Barnes's work. Barnes noted some years ago that pupils do not behave as an homogeneous group when participating in classroom discourse: they have distinctive identities as learners. He also argued that, given the right context in terms of task and pedagogic approach, all children are capable of exploratory talk as a means of taking an active part in learning. Thirty years on this argument is still highly relevant, and particularly so in the context of school mathematics. In their chapter, Solomon and Black show how pupils take on different learner identities and ways of engagement through their participation and non-participation in classroom discourse. While some pupils develop an identity of exclusion from mathematics, others more readily develop identities of engagement, which involve hypothesising and posing questions for oneself, exploring and investigating ideas, negotiating and justifying solutions to problems and using the teacher as a resource. Like Barnes, they locate the source of these differences in the interaction patterns that pupils experience. They conclude that although some pupils regularly experience what we might call dialogic interactions, which enable them to 'talk themselves into understanding', others experience heavily controlled interactions in which they adopt a largely passive role. Key to this difference is the strong emphasis on ability and attainment, which impacts on both the ways that teachers communicate with pupils and pupils' understanding of the learning process.

Robin Alexander's chapter, 'Culture, Dialogue and Learning: Notes on an Emerging Pedagogy', summarises his work on the 'emerging pedagogy' of the spoken word. He considers how it might be possible to exploit the power of talk to shape children's thinking and to secure their engagement, learning and understanding during the developmentally critical years when they are in primary or elementary schools. Alexander draws mainly on three elements of his research over the past two decades: first, a long-term comparative study of the relationship between culture and pedagogy in five countries (England, France, India, Russia and the USA) second, subsequent development work on classroom talk and specifically the idea of 'dialogic teaching'; third, observational research in UK classrooms, which preceded both of these and which ignited his desire to discover whether the identified features and problems of British pedagogy were universal or whether radical alternatives were available. Much of his work originates in classrooms, with what happens there in normal rather than ideal circumstances, and he outlines his current perspective on dialogic teaching as teachers in various parts of the UK are trying to apply it. Alexander also presents some interim findings from the schools involved in the dialogic teaching development projects, both positive and problematic.

Crossing the Atlantic again, 'Talking Texts into Being: On the Social Construction of Everyday Life and Academic Knowledge in the Classroom', introduces the work of Judith Green, Beth Yeager and Maria Castanheira, and their exploration of how knowledge is socially constructed in the classroom. Drawing on ethnographic research with students from diverse linguistic backgrounds, Green, Yeager and Castanheira describe how teachers work with students to construct a common language of the classroom, and how this shapes what counts as academic knowledge and practice. They also outline how such knowledge is 'talked into being' from the first moments of school, across time, and how this discourse shapes the ways of knowing, being and doing experienced by students in the classroom. Using specific examples drawn from the teaching of mathematics, they focus on how a teacher will use talk to guide a student's participation, and how new ways of being a mathematician are created in a bilingual 5th grade class.

In his chapter, 'Teachers' Use of Feedback in Whole-class and Group-based Talk', Frank Hardman discusses how the pedagogy of dialogic teaching challenges the thinking in government policy on education and relates this to the recent introduction of a range of 'top-down' initiatives to change pedagogic practice, with a greater emphasis on whole-class 'interactive' teaching in both primary and secondary schools in England. Drawing upon his own work, and that of a range of researchers into classroom talk (for example, Robin Alexander, Neil Mercer, and Gordon Wells in this volume), Hardman argues that the term 'dialogic teaching' should replace both the vagueness of 'interactive' and the organisational restrictiveness of 'whole-class teaching'. Dialogic teaching draws on the theoretical work of Vygotsky and Bakhtin, and also significantly upon the earlier research of Douglas Barnes. Dialogic teaching is seen as being collective, supportive and reciprocal, through the sharing of ideas and alternative viewpoints; and cumulative, in group-based and whole-class situations, with teachers and pupils building on each other's ideas and chaining them into coherent lines of thinking and enquiry. Hardman suggests that when teachers provide feedback which asks pupils to expand on their thinking, to justify or clarify their opinions, or make connections to their own experiences, this can enhance levels of pupil participation and engagement and lead to higher levels of pupil achievement. When such high-level feedback occurs, a teacher ratifies the importance of a pupil's response and allows it to modify or affect the course of the discussion in some way, weaving it into the fabric of an unfolding exchange. They chain together teacher questions and pupil responses so that the discourse gradually takes on a more collaborative quality with teacher and pupils taking turns in speaking, thereby encouraging more pupil-initiated ideas and responses and consequently promoting higher-order thinking.

In 'Reflections on the Study of Classroom Talk', Courtney Cazden explores current ideas about how talk unites what children draw from the social relationships they make in the classroom, and what they actually learn while in school. Cazden draws upon the work of Barbara Rogoff's three planes of analysis (cognitive – talk – social) to review work with middle school literacy classes that formed part of the 'Fostering a Community of Learners' (FCL) programme first initiated by Ann Brown and Joseph Campione in the early 1990s. Cazden uses interviews she conducted (with a member of the FCL team, Marty Rutherford) in 2004, with adults now in their twenties, to understand how these different planes of interaction were realised in the classroom. Cazden notes that there are strong echoes in these interviews of how these adults, then children, 'worked on understanding' (as explained by Barnes in this volume), becoming socialised into a pattern of social interaction which involved setting up starting points for their work (benchmarking), documenting and exchanging research ideas (research rotations), and talking to teachers about their ideas, as well as exchanging these ideas across and within their groups (reciprocal teaching). Cazden suggests that an 'enacted' curriculum, within which pupils explain to each other and their teacher what they have learned, effectively harnesses the power of talk for clarifying in the minds of pupils just what they do and don't understand. She concludes that the FCL programme is effective because it draws upon the individual, cognitive elements of pupils' understanding and uses talk to situate these ideas in a 'social reality' realised through collaboration, compromise and constant reassessment.

In the final chapter, 'Exploratory Talk and Dialogic Inquiry', Gordon Wells and Tamara Ball build upon Barnes's argument that 'learning is never passive' and upon his concept of exploratory talk as a fundamental tool that learners can use to actively 'work on understanding'. They propose that exploratory talk is important to the development of understanding for at least three reasons: it affords learners a sense of ownership over their own learning; it affords the feeling of being understood; and, finally, it can be internalised to mediate learners' understanding and problem solving. Wells and Ball provide evidence from their research to support claims that exploratory talk (or dialogue) promotes essential educational opportunities for students as they attempt to construct knowledge together and to make the interpretative connections involved in individual understanding. Finally, they consider the sorts of educational goals that can be served by that kind of dialogue. On the basis of their research using observational data from elementary to university classrooms, Wells and Ball argue that inquiry is a pedagogic approach that is particularly conducive to the creation of the goals and conditions that facilitate exploratory talk and inspire learners to 'try out new ways of thinking that are disturbingly different from what they are used to' (Barnes, this volume).

The contributors to this book have carried out their work in a variety of school settings, in various parts of the world. Most of them have not worked together on joint projects, yet the common message that emerges here is clear. To ensure that children are given the best opportunities for gaining an education from the time they spend in school, it is necessary to focus on how spoken language is used in the classroom. These chapters show that we have the practical knowledge needed to improve the quality of classroom talk. Yet, in most classrooms, and in most educational policy, talk remains a taken-for-granted feature of everyday life.

We and our fellow contributors are proud to follow Douglas Barnes in the study of classroom dialogue. Although most of the chapters in this book are based on very recent classroom research, the influence of his distinctive contribution to this field of enquiry is apparent in all of them. We offer this celebratory volume in the expectation that readers will also appreciate the lasting relevance of his work to the practical study of education, and in the hope that – for the benefit of pupils everywhere – policy makers and practitioners will act upon its message.

1

Exploratory Talk for Learning

Douglas Barnes

Summary

Barnes begins by outlining a 'constructivist' view of the nature of learning, and explores its implications for teaching, including the idea that coming to terms with new knowledge requires 'working on understanding' which can most readily be achieved through talk. Two kinds of talk, 'exploratory' and 'presentational', contribute to learning, but each has a different place in the sequence of lessons. Since learning in schools is a social activity, the discussion of learning moves from the individual to the group. A distinction is made between 'school knowledge' and 'action knowledge', and teachers are advised to consider whether their pupils' conception of the nature of learning is appropriate. The chapter concludes with the discussion of some practical implications for teachers.

For Discussion

1 What are the main elements in the view of learning called 'constructivism'?
2 How must these elements be modified to take account of a 'social constructivist' perspective?
3 What are the practical implications for teaching these views of learning?

(Continued)

(Continued)

4 How can 'exploratory' and 'presentational' uses of language in lessons be distinguished from one another? At what point in a scheme of teaching is each likely to be appropriate?

5 In what ways can some pupils' preconceptions about the nature of learning prove to be unproductive? What might be done about this?

6 In what ways might the distinction between 'school knowledge' and 'action knowledge' be relevant to teachers in their work?

In this chapter I shall summarise something of what I have learnt from my years as a schoolteacher and as a researcher about how pupils learn in school and how teachers can best help them. During my years in the University of Leeds I set out to investigate what role spoken – and written – language can at best play in young people's learning in classrooms and laboratories, though later on I came to define the issues less in terms of language and more as the kinds of access to the processes of learning that teachers made possible. The communication system that a teacher sets up in a lesson shapes the roles that the pupils can play, and goes some distance in determining the kinds of learning that they engage in. Thus I shall deal not only with pupils' learning but also with what teachers do to influence this. I want to acknowledge, however, that a teacher's attention is not given solely to the content of what is being taught; it is also necessary to manage social relations in the classroom, and failure in this latter respect will endanger any progress in learning. The management of these two responsibilities – which can at times seem almost to be in conflict – is central to the skill of teaching.

My own years as a schoolteacher have taught me that learning is never truly passive. One often hears the phrase *active learning* used with approval, so it is worth considering what exactly is being approved. When is learning active, and what processes does active learning include? Being 'active' does not imply moving about the room or manipulating objects (though either of these might be involved), but rather attempting to interrelate, to reinterpret, to understand new experiences and ideas. Whatever teaching method a teacher chooses – question and answer, guided discovery, demonstration or something else – it will always be the pupil who has to do the learning. He or she will make sense of the lessons only by using the new ideas, experiences or ways of thinking in order to reorganise his or her existing pictures of the world and how it can be acted upon. This is partly a matter of relating the new ideas to what a learner already knows. It is only the learner who can bring the new information, procedures or ways of understanding to bear upon existing ideas, expectations and ways of thinking and acting. That is, the learner actively *constructs* the new way of understanding.

The central contention of this view of learning, which is nowadays called 'constructivism', is that each of us can only learn by making sense of what happens to us in the course of actively constructing a world for ourselves. One implication of this is that learning is seldom a simple matter of adding bits of information to an existing store of knowledge – though some adults will have received that idea of learning from their own schooling. Most of our important learning, in school or out of it, is a matter of constructing models of the world, finding out how far they work by using them, and then reshaping them in the light of what happens. Each new model or scheme potentially changes how we experience some aspect of the world, and therefore how we act on it. Information that finds no place in our existing schemes is quickly forgotten. That is why some pupils seem to forget so easily from one lesson to the next: the material that was presented to them has made no connection with their models of the world. This implies that retrieving and transforming what we already know is a crucial part of learning.

It was Piaget who pointed out that new knowledge and experience can be *assimilated* when they fit comfortably into our existing schemes for understanding the world, but that other new ideas, that do not fit, force us to *accommodate* them by changing our schemes (Piaget and Inhelder, 1969). So some new ideas, experiences or information will require a radical revision of some part of our view of the world, and this we sometimes resist. To take one classroom example. When a teacher passed a beaker of cold water through a Bunsen flame, many of his pupils thought the droplets of water that appeared on it had either condensed from the air or spilt over the edge, both of these being familiar ideas. It required a major accommodation of their ideas about the relationship of water and fire to take in the idea that these droplets were a chemical product of the burning of the coal gas. Much of school learning requires an equally radical revision of our pictures of the physical or social world and how it works.

Since we learn by relating new ideas and ways of thinking to our existing view of the world, all new learning must depend on what a learner already knows. When we are told something we can only make sense of it in terms of our existing schemes. A child who has had no experience of blowing up balloons or pumping up bicycle tyres will make much less sense of a lesson on air pressure, however clearly it is presented, than a child who has had such experience. Most learning does not happen suddenly: we do not one moment fail to understand something, and then the next moment grasp it entirely. To take another example, compare a child's understanding of electricity with that of an adult. A child may well use the word correctly, but may lack the ability to analyse and explain, as well as to make links with those purposes and implications which make electricity important. The difference between the child and the adult will be even more marked for those who have studied physics. Most of our systems of ideas – call them schemes, frames, models, or concepts – go through a history of development in our minds, some of them changing continually throughout our lives.

The *constructivist* view of learning carries with it a radical requirement for teachers since it implies that their central task is to set up situations and challenges that will encourage their pupils to relate new ideas and ways of thinking to existing understandings and expectations in order to modify them. I find it useful to think of this as *working on understanding*. Working on understanding is, in essence, the reshaping of old knowledge in the light of new ways of seeing things. (Of course, 'seeing' here is a metaphor for various ways of symbolising, not just visual ones.) Only pupils can work on understanding: teachers can encourage and support but cannot do it for them. In this reshaping, pupils' 'old' knowledge is as important as the new experiences that are to challenge it. It is this challenge that provides the dynamic for the *accommodation*, the changing of previous ways of understanding for new ones. Adults and children alike are not always ready to make such adjustments and sometimes cling to views of the world that are familiar but are also ineffective or even untrue. It can be uncomfortable to have to change our ideas about how things are or how we should behave or interpret the world about us.

There are various ways of working on understanding, appropriate for different kinds of learning. Teachers commonly ask pupils to talk or write in order to encourage this, but drawings and diagrams, numerical calculations, the manipulation of objects, and silent thought may also provide means of trying out new ways of understanding. At the centre of working on understanding is the idea of 'trying out' new ways of thinking and understanding some aspect of the world:

this trying out enables us to see how far a new idea will take us, what it will or will not explain, where it contradicts our other beliefs, and where it opens up new possibilities.

The readiest way of working on understanding is often through talk, because the flexibility of speech makes it easy for us to try out new ways of arranging what we know, and easy also to change them if they seem inadequate. Not all kinds of talking (or writing) are likely to contribute equally to working on understanding. A great deal of the writing that goes on in school is a matter of imitating what other people have said or written, and the same is true at least in part of the talk.

It is clearly important to consider what kinds of discussion contribute most to working on understanding. When young people are trying out ideas and modifying them as they speak, it is to be expected that their delivery will be hesitant, broken, and full of dead-ends and changes of direction. This makes their learning talk very different from a well-shaped presentation such as a lecture. For this reason I found it useful to make a distinction between *exploratory talk* which is typical of the early stages of approaching new ideas, and *presentational talk* (Barnes, 1976/1992). Exploratory talk is hesitant and incomplete because it enables the speaker to try out ideas, to hear how they sound, to see what others make of them, to arrange information and ideas into different patterns. The difference between the two functions of talk is that in presentational talk the speaker's attention is primarily focused on adjusting the language, content and manner to the needs of an audience, and in exploratory talk the speaker is more concerned with sorting out his or her own thoughts.

I can illustrate exploratory talk by quoting a short extract from the recording that in 1970 first challenged me to think about its nature and functions (Barnes, 1976/1992). Four 11-year-old girls were talking about a poem that they had read. They were discussing what would happen if, as in the poem, a pupil fell asleep in class.

Anne: Well the teacher's bound to notice.

Beryl: Yes really ... because I mean ... I mean if ...

Carol: Or she could have gone out because someone had asked for her or something ... She probably felt really sorry for him so she just left him ... The teachers do ...

Anne: What really sorry for him ... so she'd just left him so they could stick pins in him. *[Tone of horrified disbelief.]*

Dinah:	Oh no she probably ... with the 'whispered' ... said 'whispered' ...
Beryl:	Yes.
Carol:	Yes but here it says ... um ... *[rustling paper]* ... Oh 'Stand away from him children. Miss Andrews stooped to see.'
Beryl:	Mm.
Anne:	So you'd think that she would do more really.
Beryl:	Yes ... you'd think she'd um ... probably wake ... if she would really felt sorry for ... sorry for him she'd ...
Dinah:	She'd wake him.
Beryl:	*[continuing]* ... wake him.
Carol:	Oh no! .... No, she wouldn't send him home alone ... because ... nobody's ...
Anne:	His mother's bad.

Although many of the contributions were disjointed and hesitant, the girls were undoubtedly sorting out their thoughts and making sense of the poem, and a few moments later arrived at an insight crucial to its understanding. The broken utterances, the changes of direction, the corrections of themselves and one another, even the disagreements, all were part of their struggle to assign meaning to the poem. The talk, for all its incompleteness, seemed to be enabling the girls to use their existing knowledge of people and behaviour to construct a meaning for the words of the poem. Soon after making this recording I began to realise that it was not only in reading literature that we need to bring existing knowledge to give meaning to what we hear or read. All understanding depends on this, whether in school or elsewhere. This encouraged me to gather material from other parts of the school curriculum that would throw light on how putting ideas into words contributes to learning.

Exploratory talk provides an important means of working on understanding, but learners are unlikely to embark on it unless they feel relatively at ease, free from the danger of being aggressively contradicted or made fun of. Presentational talk, on the other hand, offers a 'final draft' for display and evaluation: it is often heavily influenced by what the audience expects. Presentational talk frequently occurs in response to teachers' questions when they are testing pupils' understanding of a topic that has already been taught. It also occurs when anyone, child or adult, is speaking to a large or unfamiliar audience. Such situations discourage exploration: they persuade the speaker to focus on getting it right, on 'right answers' – providing expected information and an appropriate form of speech.

Much of the talk that teachers invite from pupils is presentational in nature, and it is not my intention to deny the value to learners of having to order ideas and present them explicitly to an audience. Teachers should, however, consider at what point in the sequence of learning this should take place. In my view many teachers move towards presentational talk (and writing) too soon, when pupils are still at the stage of digesting new ideas. In the earlier stages of a new topic, it is likely to be exploratory talking and writing that will contribute more to the interrelating of old ways of thinking and new possibilities: in other words, they will be more likely to enable learners to 'work on understanding'. Requiring presentational reports, spoken or written, before pupils have come to terms with new ideas is to ask for confused speech or writing. Both presentational and exploratory talk are important in learning. Teachers need to be sensitive to the differences between them and use them appropriately.

In teaching both adolescents and adults I made much use of small-group discussion as an element in an overall pattern of learning, partly because it makes it more likely that a larger proportion of a class will be actively involved in thinking aloud. However, I do not want to over-emphasise small groups in spite of the role they played in my investigations. I was often more interested in finding out how young people use talk as a tool of thinking in the absence of adult guidance than in recommending small-group methods. It is important not to allow ourselves to idealise group discussion: it is a valuable resource in a teacher's repertoire but it is not a universal remedy. Not all group discussions are as successful as the poem discussion quoted above: the very presence of a researcher with a tape-recorder encourages young people to put on a show. Group discussion should also never be seen as a *laissez-faire* option. Successful group work requires preparation, guidance and supervision, and needs to be embedded in an extended sequence of work that includes other patterns of communication. With new classes some instruction in the ground rules may be needed. (Neil Mercer and Lyn Dawes in this volume discuss an approach called 'Thinking Together' intended for this purpose, and Courtney Cazden describes an approach called 'Fostering a Community of Learners' which had been strikingly successful.) By early adolescence some young people have already developed considerable social abilities, no doubt from sharing in the life of a family and the activities of other groups as well as from school. However, the ability to think aloud and to share thoughts with others is not universal, and is not necessarily linked to academic intelligence. Some young people need help to develop these skills and even to discover what *discussion* is.

I do not want to seem to suggest that class discussions led by the teacher are less important than group work. On the contrary, they are essential. It is important, however, for teachers to make it possible for pupils to think aloud even when they are talking with the whole class. This is difficult, as every teacher knows, since in a lively class the competition to hold the floor will discourage extended speech. Moreover, pupils competing for attention do not always listen to and reply to one another's contributions, and it is part of the task of the skilled teacher to persuade them to do so. There are other problems as well. One unpredicted outcome of several small-scale studies of teachers in action was that it is surprisingly difficult for teachers to achieve insight into pupils' thinking merely by asking a question and listening to their brief answers (Barnes, 1976/1992). As a result, they may fail to grasp what pupils had been thinking and what would give them useful support. Thus their contribution to the discussion can sometimes be less than helpful in advancing their pupils' thinking. Teaching is by no means easy.

Setting up a supportive context for learning during lessons is central to good teaching. It is through talking over new ideas with their teachers and peers that pupils can most readily move towards new ways of thinking and feeling. Indeed, for many learners the support of a social group is essential. The term *common knowledge* (Edwards and Mercer, 1987; Mercer, 1995) reminds us that the construction of knowledge is essentially a social process. How teachers behave in lessons, and particularly how they receive and use their pupils' written and spoken contributions, is crucial in shaping how pupils will set about learning and therefore what they will learn. It is by the way that a teacher responds to what a pupil offers that he or she *validates* – or indeed fails to validate – that pupil's attempts to join in the thinking. In an inquiry called 'Interpretation and Transmission' I found that the way teachers interact with their pupils is closely linked to their preconceptions about the nature of the knowledge that they are teaching (Barnes and Shemilt, 1974). If they see their role as simply the transmission of authoritative knowledge they are less likely to give their pupils the opportunity to explore new ideas.

This previous paragraph illustrates an alternative tradition in the psychology of learning called *social contructivism*. This represents learners as essentially social beings who are being inducted into cultural practices and ways of seeing the world that are enacted by the groups to which they belong. (The social constructivist view of learning is also discussed by Frank Hardman on pages 131–47 of this volume.) Even what we call 'first-hand experience' is partly shaped by the meanings available in the culture we participate in. Learners must indeed 'construct' their models of the world, but the models they construct are not arbitrary; the experiences on which they are based do not come from nowhere. They are responses to activities and talk that they have shared with other members of the community, many of them older. This tradition provides a useful counterbalance to what I have written in earlier paragraphs from a more individualistic (Piagetian) perspective. Exploratory talk does not provide new information. When learners 'construct' meanings they are manipulating what is already available to them from various sources, exploring its possibilities, and seeing what can and cannot be done with it.

Vygotsky (1962) was one of the first psychologists to acknowledge the role of talk in organising our understanding of the world: he would not have dissented from this social constructivist view of learning. He insisted that our ability to talk and think is in the first instance social and only later becomes individual. By participating in activities and talk, children come to make as their own the purposes, practical categories and ways of going about things that are essential to their social environment, to their families and to the other groups they belong to. Central to this learning is speech – not just the forms of words and sentences that we all learn to use, but more importantly the meanings and purposes that they represent, and the social relationships in which they are embedded. We learn to participate not only in activities but also in the meanings which inform them.

This brings us to a paradox that underlies all deliberate teaching. School learning is at once social and individual. Our culture offers to young learners powerful ways of understanding and influencing the world, so that much learning is a matter of 'getting inside' an adult view of the world in order to use it for thinking and acting. Schools provide for pupils the opportunity of partially sharing the teacher's perspective, for successful lessons build up cumulatively a set of meanings that it is the task of each pupil to make his or her own. Each must deal with new experiences that challenge existing schemes and pictures of the world, for only he or she has access to the particular preconceptions and misunderstandings which need to be reflected on and modified. One of the challenges that face all teachers is how to help pupils to try out new ways of thinking that may be disturbingly different from what they are used to, and at the same time to give more responsibility to those learners to develop their own understanding of the matter. Courtney Cazden (2001: 22) puts the teacher's dilemma precisely: 'How to validate a student's present meaning, often grounded in personal experience, while leading the child into additional meanings, and additional ways with words for expressing them that reflect more public and educated forms of knowledge.' Teachers teach classes but pupils learn as individuals, each constructing slightly different versions of the meanings made available during the interchanges shared by the whole class and the teacher. Both the shared construction and the individual struggle to reinterpret are essential.

Some learning in schools takes place tacitly at first. Bruner (1966) showed that we often achieve conscious control only after we have gained unreflective mastery. Edwards and Mercer (1987) illustrated how primary school teachers involve their pupils in activities and talk about them in such a way as to direct attention to the crucial features that they will need to be aware of in order to participate in similar activities. It is important that such learning should later be reflected on and made explicit. Once we have laid out clearly what we believe to be the case, we are able to look critically at our assumptions and determine whether we wish to stand by them. Reflection, including the reflection that is enabled by *talk outside the event* – recollected in tranquillity, as it were – seems to be an essential prerequisite for critical thinking and the modification of what we believe.

Abstractions such as 'active learning' are likely to leave many teachers asking themselves how these ideas can be enacted in lessons. When one says that learning needs to be 'active', it implies that the learner is at least as important as the teacher in determining the success of lessons. One would want students to get into the habit of asking themselves – or the teacher – questions such as the following.

> If that is the case, how come so-and-so happens?
>
> I don't get that. What do you mean by —A—?
>
> Is —X— an example of what you're saying?
>
> If you changed —Y— (one of the elements in the statement or situation) would you get the same result?
>
> Is it like —Z—? (i.e. suggesting an analogy)

Questions such as these might be directly modelled by the teacher's practice during lessons, but more important would be the overall way in which ideas were presented and discussed in those lessons. The learner's preconceptions about what activities constitute 'learning' play an important part in this. Our society offers to young people various visions of what learning might be, including quiz shows, *Mastermind*, spelling tests, and other images which represent learning as rote memory and 'getting the right answer'. Pupils whose approach to school work is dominated by such images are likely to adopt unsuitable strategies when they are required to understand complex ideas either in science or in the humanities and social studies.

This was the central concern of a group of teachers in one Australian secondary school who decided that their pupils' preconceptions about learning were proving a major barrier. One teacher found that pupils came in and automatically copied into their notebooks whatever was on the blackboard, whether or not it was relevant or even made sense. A teacher of English, trying to encourage pupils to approach all stories with imagination, understanding and insight, was faced by pupils who wanted her to write down her questions about one particular story and provide answers so that they could learn them by heart. Clearly they had no idea of what was required. Science teachers found that pupils were memorising the words of scientific principles, instead of trying to understand them, and similarly throughout the curriculum. These teachers set up in their school a Project for Enhancing Effective Learning (PEEL), trying out various ways of helping their pupils to understand what kind of learning is required by a modern curriculum as a way of making them more effective learners (Baird and Mitchell, 1986). They were much helped in this by John Baird, who had previously carried out research into how highly intelligent and successful adult learners set about learning. He found that good adult learners, instead of narrowly committing information to memory:

1 relate new ideas, experiences and information to a wide range of existing knowledge and experiences;

2 look critically at these relationships, noticing where there are matches or discrepancies, and asking questions about these;

3 realise which parts of the new they have not fully grasped, think through the implications, and look for examples and counter-examples.

That is, they actively try to make sense of what they are learning, and relate it to what they already know and understand. This helped the PEEL teachers to decide what practical measures they should adopt to improve their students' learning. These included:

- having students write about and discuss what they already know of the topic;

- getting them to predict; 'What do you think would happen if .....? Why?';

- encouraging the asking of 'good questions' i.e. those that seek underlying principles;

- setting up frequent occasions for interpretive discussion;

- teaching the making of notes through collaborative discussion;

- encouraging students occasionally to list what they understand and what they do not yet understand;

- at times, allowing students to negotiate learning tasks.

Students can be encouraged to contribute examples, make connections with their own experience, and discuss areas where the new material seems to clash with what they thought to be the case. Discussion and explanation *by the pupils* should be a central part of lessons, and this should also include the producing and evaluating of supportive evidence. Pupils should be expected to ask questions as well as to answer them; their questions not only engage them in productive thinking but can provide valuable information to the teacher about their level of comprehension. They should learn also that some questions are more productive than others. They should be encouraged to raise problems, to propose anomalies, and to look for contexts in which the new ideas do not seem to apply as well as those in which they seem to be useful.

It is not easy to spell out in greater detail what this strategy amounts to since it depends in part on the material being taught and on the pupils, and often on contextual influences that are outside of a teacher's control. A few general suggestions can however be made. The provision of useful material for discussion – demonstrations, apparatus, maps, pictures, texts – and a habit of inviting pupils to predict and justify their predictions will let them know that thinking aloud is valuable. Teachers' questions that open lines of thought are more valuable than those which require bits of information. Listening to and reading attentively what pupils say or write, and validating their attempts to understand by replying to them, are important: teachers sometimes automatically assess when they would do better to reply. When written work is set there should often be explicit discussion of the criteria by which it is to be assessed.

When my students and I first tape-recorded lessons, we were all surprised at how much talking teachers did and how little time was left for pupils' answers. We were also amazed by the pupils' passivity: they seemed not to be engaging with the ideas being presented to them (Barnes, 1969). The question and answer routine (often called 'recitation' in the USA, and 'IRF' in several chapters of this book) performs the function of managing the class and holding their attention but it does not easily give opportunities for pupils to work on understanding through talk. Well managed, it can enable a teacher to lead a class through a complex sequence of thought, but then each pupil needs to recreate the sequence in his or her own terms. More recent commentators have insisted that IRF teaching is essential, and have shown how it can lead to developed discussion and not merely a recapitulation of authoritative material (Wells, 1993; Cazden, 2001: 41; Alexander, 2004).

Since our culture provides misleading models, it is useful to engage pupils in an explicit discussion of what learning requires of them. They should be encouraged to take an active responsibility for the progress of their learning, to identify areas of uncertainty and confusion and look for help with them. Teachers in the PEEL project found it helpful to have pupils evaluate their own strategies for learning, which was possible because they had previously discussed what constituted good learning. In effect, since learners are best placed to map the progress of new understanding, it is they who should identify what help they need. The overall purpose should be to hand over to pupils more responsibility for their own learning, by requiring them to think about it and by avoiding the mere rehearsal of inert information.

It has perhaps become too much a truism that learning is more effective when a learner perceives that what is being learnt is relevant to his or her life, though it also remains true that some young people are more likely to struggle to make sense of new experiences when these are important in their own lives. However, Phil Scott on page 31 of this volume argues persuasively that there are occasions when pupils can be persuaded to recognise the interest and challenge of subject matter they had not previously thought about. When young people feel that what is being taught in school is neither interesting nor relevant to their present and future lives they will at best receive it superficially. By 'superficially' I mean that the knowledge – of whatever kind – will not be integrated into the learner's picture of the world as he or she experiences it. In contrast, knowledge that has been integrated will have the capacity to affect how he or she thinks, feels and acts, in school or elsewhere. I found it useful to label this distinction *school knowledge* versus *action knowledge* (Barnes, 1976/1992). New knowledge is all the more powerful if it is provided just at the moment when learners realise that they need it to solve a problem or answer a question. Knowledge that answers a question that has not yet been asked will soon be forgotten. Part of a teacher's task in managing learning is the provoking of a questioning habit of mind, seeing to it that their pupils perceive that there is a question to be answered before they head them towards the material that can be used to answer it.

Too much of what is taught in school remains 'school knowledge', divorced from pupils' lives and remaining at the surface of the mind, never penetrating to any depth. When boys and girls relate new ideas to their lived-in world this is one aspect of what I mean by 'working on understanding', but of course their lived-in world is not merely the world of everyday incidents. Courtney Cazden in pages 151–83 of this volume shows how powerfully a social context for learning that empowers the learners by involving them in inquiry can generate interest in new material as well as satisfaction in the quality of their own participation.

As the years passed I became more and more convinced that learners should be given more access to the grounds upon which the knowledge they were learning was based. Knowledge is too often presented as if it is beyond challenge and beyond the examination of alternatives. Tasks are often set without teachers indicating in terms that learners can understand what criteria will be used to judge success or failure. I am convinced not only that conscious participation in learning is essential, but also that in order to achieve active learning learners should be encouraged to be *reflective* and *critical*. These concepts mark the culmination of what I have written in this chapter. They imply that every school pupil should eventually take deliberate responsibility for learning and its relationship to the world of understandings, beliefs and values that he or she inhabits. Reflection includes taking responsibility for finding connections and examples, asking questions, reinterpreting experience, and searching for new techniques and new ways of understanding relevant to the matter in hand. 'Critical' learning goes further and implies that teachers should encourage pupils to find alternative ways of looking at topics, and should help them to grasp what evidence may be used to support one or another viewpoint. The purpose is to prepare for life outside school by giving pupils the opportunity to make informed choices, and to prepare them as future adults to become full participants in their own lives.

References

Alexander, R. (2004) *Towards Dialogic Teaching: Rethinking Classroom Talk.* York: Dialogos.

Baird, J.R. and Mitchell, I.J. (eds) (1986) *Improving the Quality of Teaching and Learning: An Australian Case Study.* Clayton, Victoria: Monash University Faculty of Education.

Barnes, D. (1969) 'The language of the secondary classroom', in D. Barnes, J.N. Britton and H. Rosen (eds), *Language, the Learner and the School.* Harmondsworth: Penguin.

Barnes, D. (1976/1992) *From Communication to Curriculum.* Harmondsworth: Penguin. (Second edition, 1992, Portsmouth, NH: Boynton/Cook-Heinemann.)

Barnes, D. and Shemilt, D. (1974) 'Transmission and interpretation', *Educational Review, 26: 3.* (Reprinted in *Language Perspectives (1982)* B. Wade (ed.). London: Heinemann.)

Bruner, J.S. (1966) *Toward a Theory of Instruction.* Cambridge, MA: Belknap.

Cazden, C.B. (2001) *Classroom Discourse: the Language of Teaching and Learning.* Portsmouth, NH: Heinemann.

Edwards, D. and Mercer, N. (1987) *Common Knowledge: The Development of Understanding in the Classroom.* London: Methuen.

Mercer, N. (1995) *The Guided Construction of Knowledge: Talk Amongst Teachers and Learners.* Clevedon: Multilingual Matters.

Piaget, J. and Inhelder, B. (1969) *The Psychology of the Child.* Abingdon: Routledge and Kegan Paul.

Vygotsky, L.S. (1962) *Thought and Language.* Cambridge, MA: MIT.

Wells, G. (1993) 'Reevaluating the IRF sequence', *Linguistics and Education, 5: 1–37.*

2

Talking a Way to Understanding in Science Classrooms

Phil Scott

Summary

The chapter begins by showing that the task of a science teacher is often to enable students to move from an everyday view of a physical phenomenon to a scientific one. After defining four classes of teacher–pupil interaction, Phil Scott goes on to illustrate through quotations a series of lessons concerned with the concept of 'normal force', in which students through the discussion of perceptual evidence and diagrams come to reject an everyday account in favour of a scientific one. Interpreting this sequence, he shows that the teacher's success depended both on domain-specific scientific knowledge and on their skill in managing different modes of talk appropriately. He also points out that it was the challenge of the unexplained that gained the students' interest and not 'relevance to life'.

For Discussion

1 Why should Vygotsky's distinction between everyday and scientific thinking be important to teachers?
2 What are the differences between the 'four classes of communicative approach'?

(Continued)

(Continued)

3   How might this analysis of 'communicative approaches' be used in the training of teachers?
4   What are the characteristics of 'meaningful learning'?
5   Why is the 'cumulative nature of dialogic teaching' emphasised (page 33)?

Science can be a challenging subject both to learn and, of course, to teach! Consider for example the simple event of dropping a ball from your hand. Why does the ball fall? How can we explain this phenomenon? Some might say that the ball falls, 'because you let go of it and it's heavy'. This point of view sounds reasonable and it is easy to understand what is meant. The scientific view is somewhat different. Here, things do not fall because they are heavy, things fall because of the gravitational pull of the Earth.

This example captures the distinction between 'everyday' and 'scientific' ways of talking and thinking about events. From the everyday, commonsense point of view, the explanatory focus is entirely upon the ball which has the property of 'heaviness' and it is this which makes it fall. According to the scientific perspective, the Earth is key to the event as it attracts the ball towards its centre. Just reflect on this scientific explanation for a moment: 'The Earth attracts the ball towards its centre.' How can the Earth attract the ball when it is not even in contact with it? Our everyday experience is one of contact forces, where if you want to pull something you need to get hold of it. Here the Earth is able to exert a pull 'at a distance' through the force of gravity. This concept of action at a distance flies in the face of common sense and Isaac Newton himself was unsure about the idea even as he first developed it. Nevertheless, if you want to learn science then you must come to accept this way of talking and thinking about the natural world. For this particular example learning the language of science is likely to involve changing some basic assumptions about how the world works. It is likely to involve a significant ontological challenge (see Leach and Scott, 2002 (1978)).

In his seminal work on thought and language Vygotsky made the distinction between everyday and scientific ways of talking and thinking. Everyday ways develop through the informal interactions of day-to-day living. We talk about a ball falling 'because it's heavy', simply because that's how everybody talks about such things. By way of contrast, scientific views relate to disciplinary knowledge (whether in the natural sciences, or history, or economics, or whatever) which can only be acquired through some form of instruction. For example, no matter how long a novice stares at a falling ball, it is highly unlikely that they will come up with the concept of gravity.

Bearing these points in mind, learning science can be seen as coming to understand and to accept the scientific view, against a 'backdrop' of everyday ways of talking and thinking. The expectation is not necessarily that the learner gives up their everyday knowledge, but that they develop an alternative way of talking and thinking about the natural world. The concept of meaningful learning (Ausubel, 1963) is a helpful one here in that learning should ideally engage the student in making connections between everyday and scientific views, raising their awareness of any similarities and differences between the two perspectives. This kind of meaningful learning stands in contrast to rote learning, where the scientific view is committed to memory but is not integrated with existing ideas.

In this chapter a case study is presented to show how everyday and scientific views might be addressed in the ongoing discourse of a teaching sequence. The study involves a secondary school science teacher working with a class of 12- and 13-year-old students on the concept of the 'normal force'. An example of the normal force is the upward push which a table exerts on any object placed on it. For example, if a book is placed on a table, the table pushes up on the book and this upward push is the normal force. From an everyday point of view, many would claim that: 'There is no force acting on the book. How can the table make a push? The book is just sitting there.' This point of view might be one that you are inclined to go along with yourself. It is not at all obvious that the table is 'doing any pushing' nor is it evident that 'anything is being pushed around'. The book on the table example is in striking contrast with more obvious 'pushing events', such as a car that has broken down being pushed along the street where people are clearly pushing and the car is certainly moving.

The question which is of interest here concerns how a teacher might be able, through talk and other activities, to encourage meaningful learning of the concept of the normal force against a backdrop of everyday thinking. What kind of pedagogical approaches might be involved? How might these appear in the classroom? To help answer these questions I shall draw on the concept of 'communicative approach' (Mortimer and Scott, 2003) which is introduced in the following section.

Communicative approach

The communicative approach concept was developed by Mortimer and Scott (2003) and provides a perspective on *how* a teacher will work with students to develop ideas in the classroom. It is defined by characterising the talk between teacher and students along each of two dimensions: *interactive–non-interactive* and *dialogic–authoritative*.

Interactive communication is defined as allowing for the verbal participation of both teacher and students and *non-interactive* teaching involves only the teacher. Thus in interactive teaching the teacher typically engages students in a series of questions and answers, while in non-interactive teaching the teacher presents ideas in a 'lecturing' style (Mortimer and Scott, 2003).

In a *dialogic* communicative approach the teacher asks students for their points of view, at different times: asking for further details ('Oh, that's interesting, what do you mean by … '), or maybe asking other students whether they agree with the ideas or not ('Do you go along with what Julia has just said … ?'), and so on. Dialogic communication thus has resonances with Douglas Barnes's idea of 'exploratory talk', where the speaker is encouraged to 'try out ideas, to hear how they sound, to see what others make of them, to arrange information and ideas into different patterns' (Barnes, this volume, page 5). In dialogic talk there is always the attempt to acknowledge the views of others, and through dialogic talk the teacher attends to the students' points of view as well as to the school science view.

Of course there are many occasions in science lessons when a teacher is not interested in exploring students' ideas. Here the teacher focusses on the science point of view and if ideas or questions, which do not contribute to the development of the science story, are raised by students, they are likely to be re-shaped or ignored by the teacher. This kind of talk is defined as being *authoritative* in nature (Mortimer and Scott, 2003).

The two dimensions identified above can be combined to generate four ways in which a teacher might communicate with students.

Thus any episode of classroom talk can be identified as being either *interactive* or *non-interactive* on the one hand, or *dialogic* or *authoritative* on the other, thereby generating four classes of *communicative approach*.

	INTERACTIVE	NON-INTERACTIVE
DIALOGIC	A. *Interactive/Dialogic*	B. *Non-interactive/Dialogic*
AUTHORITATIVE	C. *Interactive/ Authoritative*	D. *Non-interactive/ Authoritative*

Figure 2.1 Four classes of communicative approach

The four classes can be characterised as follows (see Scott and Asoko, 2006):

(A) **Interactive/dialogic**: teacher and students consider a range of ideas.

(B) **Non-interactive/dialogic**: teacher reviews different points of view.

(C) **Interactive/authoritative**: teacher focusses on one specific point of view and leads students through a question and answer routine with the aim of establishing and consolidating that point of view.

(D) **Non-interactive/authoritative**: teacher presents a specific point of view.

The case of the normal force

The following case study focusses on a short sequence of five science lessons with a mixed ability Year 7 (students about 12-years-old) science class in a high school in a semi-rural setting in the north of England. The teacher, who we shall refer to as Mr Emerson, is a science specialist with about twenty years' teaching experience. Mr Emerson is highly regarded in the local science teacher community and is, by any standards, an expert teacher. The learning aim of the lessons was to provide an introduction to a school science view of four specific kinds of force: tension, gravity, normal force (also referred to as the 'up-push' by Mr Emerson) and friction. In relation to pedagogy Mr Emerson was keen to support meaningful learning of these concepts through a teaching intervention involving a range of communicative approaches. This study focusses on the teaching and learning of the 'normal force' theme.

Episode A (Monday): 'A starting point'

We join the class about 30 minutes after the start of the first lesson as the students are discussing three 'concept cartoons' (see Keogh and Naylor, 1999). One of the cartoons is entitled 'Bottle on a shelf' (Figure 2.2 below). It portrays four points of view about what forces might be acting on a bottle 'sitting' on a shelf:

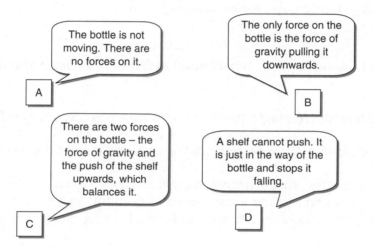

Figure 2.2   The concept cartoon: 'Bottle on a shelf'

The students first of all talked in pairs about each of these statements indicating whether they 'agree' or 'disagree' or are 'not sure' about each one. Each pair of students then worked with another pair to compare views and to reach a consensus within the group of four. Finally, the teacher gathered the class around a table at the front of the room. As we join the lesson Mr Emerson is talking to the whole class and the concept cartoon 'Bottle on a shelf' is projected onto the whiteboard:

I Teacher: Now I tell you what, if I was in one of your groups I'd have found that pretty confusing because of the number of different ideas ... Now I was over there with Josie and with Ryan and with Jordan and Kerry. Now they were looking at this and I tell you what ... they really didn't agree at all. There was a fundamental – that means a really important – disagreement. So

I'm going to ask them if they can lead off for us and just have a look at some of the ideas they talked about ...

2 Josie: Well like, I don't think that a table can push. 'cos gravity pulls, it's a force ... but a table can't push upwards, it's just in the way of the erm ... that's all.

3 Teacher: Right. Let's have a listen to what she's saying there. She's talked about the force that a lot of you have talked about, *gravity*. She's told us where she thinks that is, and what she thinks that's doing. But the disagreement between the two of them is whether the *table* can *do* anything.

Now I think when I was listening to Ryan that he was here [*points to cartoon statement C*]. That there are two forces on the bottle, the force of gravity and the push of the shelf up which balances it, and I know 'balance' is a word that a few of you were using. And I think that Josie is here [*points to cartoon statement D*], a shelf cannot push it is just in the way of the bottle and it stops it falling. Now let's use that as a starting point ...

Analysis

In this plenary Mr Emerson first of all draws attention to a 'fundamental disagreement' which had developed between two of the students, Josie and Ryan. Mr Emerson recognises that, as outlined earlier, this disagreement entails a key difference between everyday and scientific views. Mr Emerson then draws attention to the disagreement by adopting a *non-interactive/dialogic* communicative approach to review (with the help of Josie) both scientific and everyday perspectives. In doing so he pinpoints the key issue: ' ... the disagreement ... is whether the *table* can *do* anything.'

Episode B (Monday): 'Let's ask a few more people'

This episode follows on directly from the previous one as Mr Emerson asks some more students for their views:

I Teacher: Paige [*Paige has her hand up*], and please, please listen to what people are saying, 'cos it could be that they're talking about something that's going on in your mind that you want to think about.

2 Paige: It's like ... [*not audible*]

3 Teacher: So if it *wasn't* pushing up?

4 Paige: 'Cos it's like pushing it up and that's pushing it down ... [*not audible*]

5 Teacher: Yes, we've got this idea of what would happen if it *wasn't* pushing up, so you're kind of tending towards to which one? Ryan's sort of area there [*points to view C of the cartoon*]. Anybody else like to join in with this one? Zoe?

6 Zoe: I thinks it's, erm, the one where there's two forces, because there has to be something that's holding it up that stops gravity pulling it down. So erm, the table must be pushing it up in some way.

7 Teacher: You're thinking about this as logically as you can, you're saying it couldn't possibly be where it is if there wasn't something going upwards?

8 Zoe: Yeah

Five turns are missed out here in which Mr Emerson, as an aside, checks student agreement about the direction in which gravity acts, establishing that it pulls down.

13 Teacher: Anyway, so you're [*referring to Zoe*] kind of going that way [*points to view C*]. Let's ask for some more people … I mean is there anybody thinks that they'd like to talk about that? [*pointing to view A*]: 'if it's not moving there can't be any forces'. That it's not moving surely there aren't any forces on it. Zoe again?

14 Zoe: Well the force must be acting down otherwise everything would be just floating about everywhere.

15 Teacher: So you can't accept that one at all?

16 Students: No, no, no.

17 Teacher: What about this one then? [*points to view B*] The only force on the bottle is the force of gravity pulling it down. It's quite similar to that [*pointing to view C*] isn't it? Anybody else want to say any more about the bottle before we move on? George?

In the next 11 turns George, Kelly and Ryan offer ideas about what might happen with the bottle if it stands on the table for a very long period of time. Mr Emerson then draws the discussion to a close.

Analysis

Here the teacher opens the floor to the whole class. The teacher encourages contributions: *'Anybody else like to join in with this one?'*

Five students offer points of view, making relatively extended comments. The teacher refers systematically to the ideas presented in the concept cartoon but throughout offers no evaluation of the students' comments. In this way Mr Emerson encourages an *interactive/dialogic* communicative approach as the students offer a range of ideas. At this point in the lesson Mr Emerson switches attention to another cartoon: this time involving a ball hanging from a string. The issue of whether or not the table is pushing up on the bottle is left unresolved, setting up a teaching and learning 'conceptual cliffhanger' to be returned to later.

Episode C (Wednesday): 'You really argued about something on Monday'

We return to the class for the next lesson which was staged two days later. The first part of the lesson focussed on the concept of gravity, and Mr Emerson now returns to the unresolved matter from the previous lesson, the issue of whether or not a table can push up:

I Teacher:		I'd like to get you to think about one of the ideas that you really *argued* about on Monday. You really *argued* about something on Monday and you did it right at the front here and you did it in little groups. What was the idea that you were arguing about? Josie was in the middle of this and Jordan was in the middle of this argument. What were you arguing about? Josie?
2 Josie:		That a table can't push up.
3 Teacher:		Yeah … it was this argument about the table not being able to push up to support the gravity force that was pulling down on that heavy bottle. Yeah? What I want to do … I want to leave you this morning … with a picture of something that might help you to believe that that [*knocking on the table*] can push up. Now this is a very logical little argument, so you're gonna have to follow it through. To start off with, what I'd like to do is to just get Sam to put his hands on either side of this balloon and gently squeeze it together. In fact come and stand up here for me Sam [*Sam stands at front of room*] … So could you just gently, like that, push that together? [*Sam squeezes the balloon between his hands*] Now what's he doing to the shape of that, Sharon?
4 Sharon:		He's making it flatter.
5 Teacher:		Going flatter. Now you're going to have to describe this, what you're doing now [*talking to Sam*]. So just let go. What are you doing with this bottom hand, Sam?

6 Sam: Sort of like pushing it [*in quiet voice*].

7 Teacher: He says he's sort of like pushing it. But you *really are* pushing it, aren't you? That hand is pushing up at the same time as that one is pushing down [*teacher stands next to Sam and gestures up and down*]. In doing that he's changing the shape of the balloon isn't he? Now if you put that balloon on the desk now. Can everybody see? Put your hand on top there now and do the same thing [*Sam pushes down on the balloon on the desk*]. Not too hard. What's he done to the shape of the balloon there, Sean?

8 Sean: Pushing it down …

9 Teacher: He's pushing it down. What's he done to the shape?

10 Sean: Flattened it.

11 Teacher: Flattened it. Now, he's only got one hand on there at the moment. Where on Earth is the other force that's changing the *shape*? Where is the other force that is changing the shape? Let's hear a few people telling us.

12 Holly: From the table.

13 Teacher: Holly says the *table is* pushing. Levi, what do you say?

14 Levi: I think the table is pushing.

15 Teacher: The *table* is pushing. What do you say, Penny?

16 Penny: The table is pushing.

17 Teacher: You know this seems totally logical to me that if he changed the shape using two hands like that. If you take one hand away and push it down and get the same shape, something else must be pushing. What else do you think is pushing? Do you agree? [*asking Sam*]

18 Sam: [*nods yes*]

Analysis

Mr Emerson starts this episode by referring back to Monday's lesson and in particular to '*the ideas that you really argued about on Monday*'. He not only refers to the argument but also to the particular students who were involved: '*Josie was in the middle of this and Jordan was in the middle of this argument.*' There is a definite change of pace and urgency here as Mr Emerson demands the attention of the students as he provides '*a picture of something that might help you to believe that that can push up*'.

Mr Emerson enlists the help of one of the students, Sam, and presents an argument to suggest that the table *can* push up, focussing attention on the forces acting on a balloon. He achieves this over turns 3–12 by taking an *interactive/authoritative* communicative approach, played out through distinctive initiation–response–evaluation (I-R-E) patterns of three:

3 Teacher:	Now what's he doing to the shape of that, Sharon?	**[INITIATION]**
4 Sharon:	He's making it flatter.	**[RESPONSE]**
5 Teacher:	Going flatter.	**[EVALUATION]**
Teacher:	Now you're going to have to describe this, what you're doing now. So just let go. What are you doing with this bottom hand, Sam?	**[INITIATION]**
6 Sam:	Sort of like pushing it [*in quiet voice*].	**[RESPONSE]**
7 Teacher:	He says he's sort of like pushing it.	**[EVALUATION]**

This pattern of discourse continues through until Turn 12 when Holly provides the correct response that the other force is '*From the table*'. Mr Emerson then conducts rapid confirmatory exchanges (Edwards and Mercer, 1987) with Levi and Penny prior to concluding the episode with an authoritative statement in Turn 17. In this way the teacher introduces the scientific point of view to the social plane.

Episode D (Monday): 'Tomatoes in the scale pan'

In the next lesson, on the following Monday, Mr Emerson first of all introduces the idea of 'force arrows' which can be used to represent forces. He then presents the class with a number of drawings each of which shows a situation for which the students are asked to add force arrows. One of the drawings shows some tomatoes in the top-pan of a weighing balance (see below).

The students work in groups of four on their forces diagrams before Mr Emerson calls them to the front to talk through what they have been doing and to demonstrate their ideas by 'dragging' electronic force arrows into position on a copy of the drawing on the whiteboard. Paige volunteers to use the whiteboard to show the forces acting in the tomatoes example and first shows an arrow, 'gravity', pulling down on one of the tomatoes:

(A)

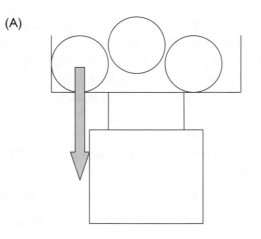

Paige knows that there is a second arrow acting upwards but is not sure about where to place it. Holly joins in and suggests to Paige that the second arrow acts upwards at the lower surface

(B)

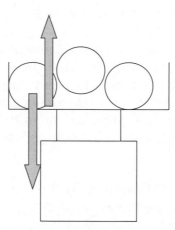

1 Teacher: So that's the precise point that the force upwards comes from. Any other points about that? Zoe? [*Zoe has her hand up*]

2 Zoe: I think it's wrong … 'cos the actual spring pushes it up.

3 Teacher: It's interesting 'cos Zoe's talking about the inside of the balance here. What were you saying is on the inside of that balance?

4 Zoe: Well … there's a spring in the middle.

5 Teacher: Hmm, interesting. 'Cos what you're saying is inside that balance is something that's pushing it back up. You're saying that spring's in the middle there?

6 Zoe: Yeah.

7 Teacher: Do you want to come and grab the pen and show us where that might be? This is quite an interesting idea.

8 Zoe: The spring's here, so the arrow should be there …

Zoe moves the upward arrow across to cover the line of the spring in the balance and some discussion follows about the exact placement of the arrow. Mr Emerson asks where the end of the arrow should be. Josie offers to help and draws in the arrow:

(C)

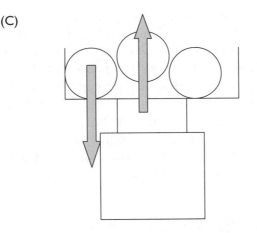

9 Josie: That's the start of the arrow and that's where the spring is.

10 Teacher: Great. And that's pushing … up?

11 Josie: Yeah.

12 Teacher: The up-push. The normal force. And what about that old gravity then?

13 Josie: It's sort of in the centre like this [*pointing to the centre of a specific tomato*].

14 Teacher: Depending on which particular tomato you choose maybe. And if we were taking all of the tomatoes together? I suppose you could just put it in the middle there?

Josie moves the upward arrow into the centre of the tomatoes so that the final diagram appears:

(D)

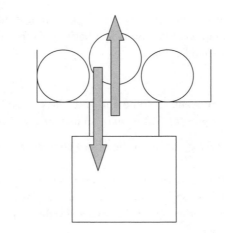

Analysis

Paige, with the assistance of Holly, draws two force arrow diagrams (A and B) which appear to be acceptable from a scientific point of view. However, Mr Emerson asks for comments and it becomes clear that Zoe has a different idea which is based on the action of the spring in the balance providing the upward force. Mr Emerson is quite open to this alternative point of view, taking an *interactive/dialogic* communicative approach, and directs Zoe to 'grab the pen and show us where that might be' (Diagram C). Josie now joins in and a more authoritative interaction with Mr Emerson (focussing on the placement of the arrows) leads to the Final Diagram D.

Episode E (Wednesday): 'What's my word?'

In this final episode on the following Wednesday Mr Emerson engages the class in a short review exercise. The exercise takes the form of a 'game' where a student volunteer comes to the front of the room and has a label, bearing a scientific word, stuck on their fore-head (sic!) by the teacher. The rest of the class provide clues to help the student guess the word (which they can't see). We join the class as Paige sits with the words 'up-push' or 'normal force' on a paper label on her forehead. Josie is the first to offer a clue:

I Josie:	The table with the bottle has this.
2 Teacher:	Josie is using a picture we've been introduced to … just give us a bit more.
3 Josie:	Like a bottle standing on a table has gravity on it and *something* keeping it up from the table.

From Josie's clue Paige correctly guesses 'normal force'.

Analysis

In providing her clue, Josie refers to the 'bottle on the table' example introduced earlier by Mr Emerson. This is precisely the example which Josie struggled with in Episode A, nine days earlier: '*Well like, I don't think that a table can push. 'Cos gravity pulls, it's a force ... but a table can't push upwards, it's just in the way of the erm ... that's all.*' Now she fluently deals with the idea as she offers a clue about the table providing a normal force.

Discussion

The analysis presented above reveals a distinctive pattern of shifts in the communicative approach around periods of whole-class and small-group activity. The teaching sequence started with two dialogic episodes (A and B) where the teacher brought to light the students' views, from the preceding small group session, on the concept cartoon 'Bottle on a shelf'. The concept cartoon proved to be a very effective 'dialogic tool', as it prompted *active* consideration of different points of view by the students. This engagement with different ideas saw some students, such as Josie and Ryan, clearly expressing what they thought and as Mr Emerson commented, 'they really didn't agree at all ... there was a fundamental disagreement'.

It is worth commenting on the fact that here we have two young people who are fully engaged in talking and thinking through the question of whether or not a shelf can exert a force. It is often argued that to engage young people in science the science content must be made relevant to their lives and interests. This case offers an alternative point of view. If a question is framed skilfully and challenges students' existing points of views then there is the potential to engage students in talking and thinking through that question, irrespective of its apparent 'relevance'. Here the relevance is invoked not through some external linkage to music, soccer or television, but by a student having an existing point of view on the question in hand and a form of intellectual relevance is thereby brought into play. In such a way the interactive/dialogic communicative approaches developed by the teacher have the potential to motivate students and to draw them into the problem.

In addition to motivating students, the initial dialogic approaches were also fundamentally important in exposing the non-trivial

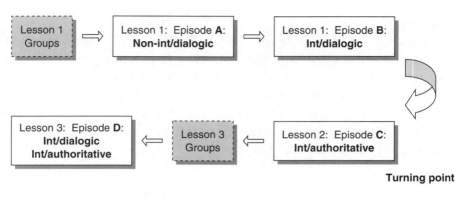

Figure 2.3   Shifts in communicative approach

nature of understanding the science involved. Supposing the teacher, in lesson 1, had simply asserted in a non-interactive/authoritative way that 'the shelf pushes up on the bottle'. With such an approach there would be no opportunity to explore differences between ideas, no encouragement to make links to existing ideas, no openness to questions such as 'How can a shelf make a force?' With such an approach there would be no apparent problem to address and therefore no questions to pose. It is clear that if meaningful learning is the desired outcome, as opposed to rote acceptance of what the teacher has said, then the teacher has the job of problematising (see Engle and Conant, 2002) the content under consideration. Mr Emerson achieved this by explicitly drawing attention to the different points of view presented in the concept cartoon and being open to students' interpretations of those views. Indeed, the teacher used the difference in opinion between Josie and Ryan as the starting point and *epistemic impetus* for this sequence of teaching.

In Episode C there was a change in pedagogy as the teacher adopted an authoritative approach in presenting the scientific view of the normal force. This shift from a dialogic to authoritative approach constitutes a 'turning point' in the sequence of episodes as the dialogic interactions were 'closed down' (Scott and Ametller, 2007) and the teacher focussed on the school science point of view.

In Episode D the students were given the opportunity to apply the normal force concept to a new context (tomatoes in the scale pan), using the arrow notation. The students were once again given time to 'try out' and to 'talk through' this new idea in small groups as they took their first steps in developing a broader understanding of the concept. When the students reported back from their group discussions a dialogic interaction was prompted by Zoe as she suggested an alternative forces arrow representation for the tomatoes in the pan. This kind of dialogic interaction, focusing on *scientific* subject matter, is far less common than those dialogic interactions which typically occur at the start of a teaching sequence and focus on the students' *everyday* views.

In this way the communicative approach shifted between dialogic and authoritative phases as the teacher attempted to support meaningful learning by first of all drawing attention to the differences between everyday and scientific views and then supporting students as they applied the concept of normal force in different contexts. In general terms, if students are invited to engage in a dialogic exploration of ideas about some phenomenon, then there must be subsequent authoritative interventions where the scientific point of view is clarified and introduced. This follows from the fact that science itself is an authoritative body of knowledge which involves accepted ways of thinking and talking about phenomena. Conversely, if scientific views are presented in an authoritative way, then time needs to be allowed for the dialogic exploration of those ideas by students. In Douglas Barnes's terms, the students need time to 'work on understanding' (Barnes, this volume, page 4). Thus, once the concept of 'normal force' had been introduced to the social plane of the classroom, the students needed the opportunity to talk through and to apply that concept for themselves (in Episode D). In such a way authoritative talk acts as a seed for dialogic exchanges and conversely dialogic talk prompts the need for authoritative intervention (Scott et al., 2006).

A further distinctive feature of this teaching sequence concerns the way in which the normal force theme was addressed and developed over an extended time line covering all five lessons. This was achieved, for example, as students referred to arguments from previous lessons and as the teacher recovered the views voiced by specific students. In these and other ways continuous thematic lines were set up throughout the sequence allowing arguments and ideas to be returned to and offering opportunities for review, consolidation and the wider application of the normal force concept. This is in contrast to a 'one-shot' pedagogical approach where new ideas are introduced and the teacher then moves on. There are resonances here with Alexander's (2004) concept of the 'cumulative' nature of dialogic teaching, whereby 'teachers and children build on their own and each other's ideas and chain them into coherent lines of thinking and enquiry' (p. 105, this volume). If meaningful learning is the desired outcome of teaching then this stretched-out-in-time character is essential, as a new scientific concept is first related to everyday views and then applied to an increasing range of contexts. In reality the time line for learning about a scientific concept such as the normal force is not restricted to five or so lessons, but will extend for as long as it remains a part of the learner's talking and thinking. There are clear implications here for a coherent approach to planning science curricula, as specific concepts are returned to and expanded in detail and application over a matter of years.

A key point relating to this temporal pattern of shifting between communicative approaches concerns the level of teacher expertise required to achieve it. This expertise is built in part on a teacher's *domain specific* knowledge and insights relating to:

- students' everyday views about a particular phenomenon;

- how individual students in *this* class think about *this* problem at *this* time;

- the detail of the scientific account and how it relates to everyday views;

- possible teaching activities to engage students in dialogue (such as concept cartoons);

- possible approaches to presenting the scientific view (such as the balloon demonstration);

- productive questions to probe students' understandings, and so on.

This knowledge is domain specific in that the insights surrounding the 'normal force' are clearly different from those relating to 'electric circuits'.

In addition, a teacher needs to have the *general* pedagogical and management skills required to put into practice all of these insights and activities with a group of 25 children. A fundamental aspect of this entails being able to develop a working atmosphere in the classroom where students feel happy and confident in expressing their views and where they will listen thoughtfully to the contributions of others and to the words of the teacher. With these points in mind, it is interesting to reflect for a moment on how Mr Emerson introduced the scientific concept of the normal force. At that point in the lesson sequence some children in the class had committed themselves to arguing that the shelf could push up, while others stated that it could not. In this context Mr Emerson chose his words carefully: 'What I want to do … I want to leave you this morning … with a picture of something that might help you to believe that *that* [*knocking on the table*] can push up.' Thus the teacher did not talk of proving some students right and others wrong, but of helping them to believe in a difficult idea. The success of this approach can at least in part be gauged by the response of Josie who was initially quite clear in stating that a table cannot push up, but by the end of the sequence had accepted the scientific point of view. Some argue that exposing students' views through dialogic interaction can lead to a negative personal response if they later prove to be at odds with the school science view. This was certainly not the case for Josie.

In conclusion, what are we able to say about how this teacher was able, through talk and other activities, to encourage meaningful learning of the normal force against a backdrop of everyday thinking? The discussion above points to a pedagogy which is based on purposeful shifts in a communicative approach as everyday and scientific views are juxtaposed and the scientific view is applied in different contexts. The teaching and learning necessarily take place over time and demand the highly-skilled guidance of the teacher, addressing both the content and affective/motivational matters, and the thinking and talking involvement of the students. Did the teaching lead to meaningful learning in this case? Evidence from the teacher's test suggests that the students had come to be able to handle the concept of normal force in familiar contexts. Furthermore, the research evidence from post-teaching interviews showed a clear student understanding of the similarities and differences between everyday and scientific views. Finally, the transcripts from these lessons offered copious evidence of students who were fully engaged in talking and thinking science.

Perhaps this outcome should not be surprising to us. Douglas Barnes has argued that '*the communication system that a teacher sets up in a lesson shapes the roles that pupils can play, and goes some distance in determining the kinds of learning that they engage in*' (Barnes, this volume, page 2). In this particular case the teacher enabled his students to occupy different epistemic roles as they at times worked dialogically on everyday and scientific ideas and at other times engaged authoritatively in formulating and applying the scientific view. By taking on these different roles the students were assisted towards the teacher's goal of meaningful learning.

References

Alexander, R. (2006) *Towards Dialogic Teaching.* York: Dialogos.

Ausebel, D.P. (1963) *The Psychology of Meaningful Verbal Learning.* New York: Grune and Stratton.

Keogh, B. and Naylor, S. (1999) 'Concept cartoons, teaching and learning in science: an evaluation', *International Journal of Science Education,* 21(4): 431–46.

Leach, J. and Scott, P. (2002) 'Designing and evaluating science teaching sequences: an approach drawing on the concept of learning demand and a social constructivist perspective on learning.' *Studies in Science Education,* 38, 115–42.

Mortimer, E.F. and Scott, P.H. (2003) *Meaning Making in Science Classrooms.* Buckingham: Open University Press.

Scott, P.H. and Ametller, J. (2007) 'Teaching science in a meaningful way: striking a balance between "opening up" and "closing down" classroom talk', *School Science Review,* 88: 324. Hatfield, UK: Association for Science Education (ASE).

Scott, P.H. and Asoko, H. (2006) 'Talk in science classrooms', in V. Wood-Robinson (ed.), *ASE Guide to Secondary Science Education.* Hatfield, UK: Association for Science Education (ASE).

Vygotsky, L.S. (1978) *Mind in Society: The Development of Higher Psychological Processes* (M. Cole, V. John-Steiner, S. Scribner and E. Souberman (eds)). Cambridge, MA: Harvard University Press.

Wells, G. (1999) *Dialogic Inquiry: Towards a Sociocultural Practice and Theory of Education.* Cambridge: Cambridge University Press.

Wertsch, J.V. (1991) *Voices of the Mind.* Cambridge, MA: Harvard University Press.

3

From Exploratory Talk to Critical Conversations

Kathryn M. Pierce and Carol Gilles

'When things change, sometimes you have to change to make them better.'

(Jordan, after reading *Dragon's Gate*)

Summary

Pierce and Gilles found exploratory talk to be a powerful way of enabling younger students to explore works of literature, and decided to extend a similar approach to develop a 'critical conversation' in which students engage with social and ethical issues that might affect their future actions. They provide details of how teachers can set up critical conversations in lessons at elementary (primary) and middle schools, and give examples of critical discussions and other outcomes. They suggest that a teacher's central task is to set up 'a culture of talk', and end with an analysis of the various kinds of talk that teachers should value.

For Discussion

1 What are the characteristics of 'critical conversation', and what is its educational significance?
2 List some of the strategies that Pierce and Gilles (and their collaborator Jean Dickinson) have found useful in setting up 'critical' versions of exploratory talk and in establishing 'a culture of talk'.

(Continued)

(Continued)

3 What conceptions of the purposes of schooling seem to be implicit in Jean Dickinson's chart of classroom talk (Figure 3.1, page 44)?

4 Describe and evaluate the understandings and insights displayed by Kathryn Pierce's middle school students in their remarks about racial discrimination and the Civil Rights Movement (pages 48 to 51).

5 What value might teachers find in being aware of the five different kinds of talk discussed under the heading 'Our Beliefs about How Talk Supports Learning'?

The opening quote for this chapter is from an 11-year-old engaged in a literature discussion group that was exploring immigration. It also serves as a kind of a metaphor for our own work, as we have shifted our interest in classroom talk from documenting reflections of learning to supporting critical conversations. We believe, like Bahktin (1981), that we are changed by each interaction with our learners, colleagues and distant teachers. Douglas Barnes, particularly in his book *From Communication to Curriculum* (Barnes, 1976), provided us with strategies for looking closely at talk and supporting the professional changes we have made.

Our interest in talk grew out of our own classrooms as we observed our students making sense of text experiences and learning. We investigated literature discussion groups as a more effective way of supporting readers than marching them through the skills list in a basal reading programme. Basal readers focus on students reading a story, answering pre-determined comprehension questions, and then completing drill and practice pages. In literature discussion groups, students have opportunities to choose a book, read and write about it, and then discuss the book in depth in a small group with others who have chosen the same title. By studying literature discussion groups, we have come to value the role of literature in promoting generative conversations, the role of talk in learning, the importance of partner and small-group experiences to support students as they work at understanding new ideas, and the important role of the teacher in creating a supportive learning environment and scaffolding the learning that occurs. During the last decade or so, we have examined Barnes's ideas more closely to better understand that the role of talk in the classroom is both a way for students to learn and a central window on to what students are working at understanding.

This chapter chronicles our growth and change as we worked to unpack and understand Barnes's idea of *exploratory talk*. Trying to understand that concept prompted us to look at classroom talk through several lenses and to identify the different types of talk that we feel are essential in those classrooms where learning is central. At the same time, we became increasingly aware of students' need to use talk to critique their worlds and then to involve others in making changes that would lead to a more just society. We named instances in which students were using talk to critique and take thoughtful new action as 'critical conversations'. We asked the question, 'What are critical conversations and how do we increase the likelihood that students will engage in them?' In telling our story, we describe the strategies we used to create spaces for various types of talk and share examples from our research in elementary and middle-level classrooms over the past ten years. Our research includes the careful study of student talk in small group literature discussions, particularly talk about books that support social critique. Excerpts from transcripts of literature discussions illustrate how teachers can create and sustain a learning environment that nurtures exploratory talk, and how they can also create spaces for critical conversations about issues of equity and social justice.

Using talk to support meaning making and address critical issues

In the following sections we describe the lessons we have learned about the kinds of talk that support meaning making and address critical issues – the talk that constitutes 'critical conversations'. The examples that follow come from Carol's work in Jean Dickinson's fifth grade classroom with 10- and 11-year-olds and Kathryn's work in her multi-age primary classroom (6- to 8-year-olds) and, later, in her middle-grade classrooms with 11- to 13-year-olds. We document the strategies that helped students engage in critical talk about the books they read, and about their world.

Creating a classroom community through talk

Community building begins by using talk to connect students to each other socially, so they begin to care about and trust each other. Both Jean and Kathryn begin each year by using talk to help students learn more about their fellow classmates. Both teachers begin partner work and small groups early on in the year and spend time helping students to get to know what is expected in a small-group setting. In addition, both teachers make their expectations clear and explain how talk works in groups. Students quickly realise that meaningful talk is an expectation in these classrooms. For example, while giving directions at the start of a work time, Kathryn will say, 'Today you're going to revisit the picture books you looked at yesterday, looking more deeply at these books and looking for ideas and patterns that cut across the books ...' Jean spends time at the end of each group processing. Students might complete a chart of 'What went well in our group' and 'When our group didn't work' so they can name the processes that are working to make the talk useful to them. Such activities then help build a 'culture of talk' in the classroom. Students know that they will be using talk to get ready, process and reflect on their learning.

Jean's expectation is that students will read excellent literature and engage with one another to explore ideas through their writing and talk (Dickinson, 1993). Throughout the school year, both teachers regularly call upon students to reflect on their use of talk, to consider the ways that talk supports their learning, and to document the ways ideas have built up over time, layer by layer, through exploratory talk with classmates.

Creating spaces for exploratory talk

Exploratory talk is essential for meaning making. Having students build on one another's ideas and create meaning together is the essence of critical conversations. Yet it is not easily achieved. We searched for ways to increase the potential of exploratory talk occurring in our classrooms.

Jean encourages exploratory talk through reading aloud from a picture book or novel. As students become more familiar with listening to and reading good books, Jean prepares her students to delve deeper into the text by considering how their talk is helping them think about the book. To engage them at a deeper level, Jean might one day read a portion of the book for students to savour it; then on the second day she may copy two or three pages of the same text for the students to reread along with her. Jean asks questions like, 'What kind of talk takes us deep?' or 'What just happened to your thinking?' to help students bring their thinking to a conscious level. As Jong, a fifth grader said, 'She returns to the passages that she wants us to think hard about.' Copying a passage or putting it on the overhead also serves to slow down the talk. Jean often asks open-ended questions such as, 'What do you notice here?' or 'What is the author doing here?' to get students to think more deeply. And then she waits. Her body language will say that she has all the time in the world for good thinking to occur. Often the silence will be broken by one voice, and then others will follow. Students are not afraid that they will be laughed at or mocked, because a strong community has been built up and continues to be nurtured. Students will then return to small, student-led discussion groups, where they will continue the deep thinking.

Kathryn also encourages her students to engage in exploratory talk, as is shown in the following example from her classroom. Sam, Tom, Colin and Jordan were discussing a text set (a thematically related set of picture books) around the theme of 'Two Cultures/Two Worlds'. Other groups had text sets relating to various themes connected to immigration experiences. The students began by sharing what they had been reading and then moved into a discussion of the connections they were making across the books in the set. The excerpt below begins with Sam sharing his observation that most of the books in their set show people having problems related to cultural differences:

S: It doesn't show all the problems going on which there is just as many problems as all the good things going on and that all the books someone's having trouble with something. Like in that book, *How My Parents Learned to Eat* (Friedman, 1987), there are two people trying to learn the other person's culture. So I think that kinda makes the reader want to go on because if everything was happy, they would think the book was kinda boring.

T: Yeah everything needs to have a problem or else there's no point in it really.

KMP: Did all the books that you found have a problem in them?

T: Well almost. They [*the books Tom looked at*] were just poems and that was just kind of a statement about something. But even them, most of them were a statement about some kind of problem so ...

S: Every book or *America Is* ... (Borden, 2002), it doesn't really have a conflict. It's just like, what I said, it only shows the important things or the good things about the book. It just doesn't show anything bad, so there's no problem. So it doesn't really spark the reader so they really want to continue on – they want to choose a different book. Yeah, that's why other books are so popular like *Lord of the Rings,* like ...

C: There's a great conflict between two worlds, I don't know ...

KMP: Within a single world?

C: I don't want to say two worlds, but two cultures, two ideas ...

J: That want their own world ...

C: What's right and who wants dominance.

T: The constant theme among these books, too, is that it's always two cultures in one area. And each of them thinking that it's kind of their birthright. But not necessarily an area, but some sort of material thing and that's the whole conflict in most of the books.

The talk in this excerpt is representative of exploratory talk as Barnes (1976/1992) defines it. The talk is hesitant and halting, with restarts. The group members talk with one another and build on one another's ideas. As the members of the group discuss the books they've been reading, they discover a pattern – all the books, or at least the interesting ones, include characters dealing with some sort of problem or conflict. The students move from sharing specific examples, or summaries, of what they've been reading to constructing a hypothesis about what happens when people representing two different cultures come together in one place or vie for control over some material thing. Colin names the pattern as 'who wants dominance' and Tom elaborates by explaining that each conflict involves at least one group that feels it is their 'birthright' to have control or dominance. The students did not come into the conversation understanding these insights – they built these new understandings through exploratory talk with one another and by making connections across the books as well as to the other information they had been learning about immigration.

Establishing this *culture of talk* in the classroom encourages exploratory and critical talk. To do this, students must feel comfortable discussing 'half-baked' ideas with their classmates. In order to push the boundaries of what they know and understand, students must be willing to work in the uncomfortable territory along those boundaries – talking through ideas that are just emerging and stopping, on occasion, to change their minds. Barnes (1976) reminds us that in a true learning community founded on exploratory talk, learners will argue with and challenge one another's ideas. Discord is a necessary part of the learning process. To engage in such difficult conversations, students must care about one another enough to want to hear their ideas, and to want to think through their own ideas within the group. To be successful, they must be willing to challenge one another. As Devontè (a student of Kathryn's) reminds us, 'I was thinking that it makes a good discussion when everybody's really into the discussion and they are debating over it ... I think when everybody has a different point of view it makes it challenging for everybody' (Wilson, 2004). Trust is an essential component in this collaborative learning community, particularly when students are challenging their own and others' world-views.

Considering new perspectives

Another way to encourage exploratory talk that leads to critical conversations is to consider new perspectives. Kathryn and Jean will invite students to consider multiple perspectives on the texts they are reading, the ideas they are exploring with others, and their own emerging understandings. The strategies they use include: making talk visible, moving across sign systems, and taking ideas to a larger audience.

Making talk visible
Talk is fleeting; it disappears quickly. Jean will help students 'slow down' the talk to make it more visible. She might say, 'Grab that idea and hold onto it. It is just out of reach,' as a student fumbles with the right wording to make his point clear. Or she might ask, 'Do you almost have it? Is it just under the surface? What can you do to see it clearly?' Such questions will help students to persevere, to make their points clear and to really listen to one another in order to piggyback on others' ideas. In addition, Jean uses webs and charts to document the ideas that students raise in their small-group and

What kind of talk takes us deep?

- Mrs D says something about the book and we start talking.
- Someone starts talking about:

  o   a part they like, don't like, a part they would change;
  o   violence and action;
  o   the emotions of the characters.

- Our ideas are on chart paper where we can see them.
- Made connections to other texts and stories.
- Talk about the author's use of symbols.
- We talk about why characters do what they do

  o   We talk about how our feelings change.
  o   Keep on talking with other people.
  o   Deciding what is right or wrong.
  o   Learning about 'Life Lessons'.
  o   Learning the ideas of others.
  o   Seeing other perspectives.
  o   Talking about someone else's story.
  o   Sharing our own stories.

Figure 3.1   One of Dickinson's classroom talk charts

whole-class discussions (see Figure 3.1 for an example of a chart). When her students are reading *Shades of Gray* (Reeder, 1989), she will ask them to think about issues where there is no 'right' or 'wrong' answer. After one lengthy, charted discussion, a student explained, 'I get inside the book and come back out of the book as a changed person.'

As Jean commented about her charting:

> I have to be really thinking through what the kids are saying – because I need to be hearing very clearly what they're saying – so that it's on the chart. That really keeps me in tune with a very conscious level of thinking. How can I take them to the next level? I don't think I realise that until I really start recording things on the chart. It helps facilitate their discussion.

Returning to the chart a day later, students will pull some of the big ideas from their chart and extend their thinking. They will chart some of the 'big questions' that they will use to dig deeper into the literature. These visual icons/symbols of the talk then support students in revisiting their ideas, in critiquing their use of talk, and in documenting the development of new insights. Both teachers occasionally audiotape and transcribe student talk, sharing these transcripts with their students so that teachers and students alike can revisit the ways talk is being used.

Moving across sign systems

While studying the American Civil Rights Movement of the 1960s, Kathryn's primary grade students spent time reading and discussing picture books that showed individuals and groups being discriminated against by others, and books that showed individuals acting on behalf of others. These young students used improvisational drama to explore the words, feelings, and responses of characters involved in an injustice or acting for change. They also wrote and dramatised their own friendship stories to show how friends can use talk to resolve conflicts. They used *sketch-to-stretch* (Short et al., 1988/1996), informal sketches that capture their responses to texts, to explore abstract ideas such as power, justice, and equity (Pierce, 2006). Moving across various sign systems – drama, writing, drawing – helped these students consider new perspectives on the texts they were reading, the ideas about equity and social justice they were beginning to understand, and their own responses to the injustices and social actions in their everyday lives. These shifts across sign systems can engage students in deeper conversations about central ideas as they move back and forth between particular and general, and between literal and abstract (Wilson, 2004; Pierce, 2006).

Taking ideas to a larger audience

When students go public with their work, they will begin to see that work from a new perspective. They will consider what they have learned or realised through their discussions. In addition, they can consider how their ideas will connect with the experiences of their audience, how to meet their audience partway, and how to lead their audience through an abbreviated version of their own learning journey. In Kathryn's middle-school classroom, thesis statements and thought-provoking questions provide effective vehicles for structuring small-group presentations as a culminating event for literature discussion groups. Students will formulate a primary thesis they want others to explore. To help audiences grapple with the ideas reflected in the thesis statements, presenters then craft one or more thought-provoking questions to stimulate a conversation. When Kathryn's students made presentations based on their reading of different immigration novels, students were called

upon to present a thesis statement and thought-provoking questions that (1) reflected the discussion/meaning-making journey of
the presenters and (2) invited the audience to reflect on their own
novels and discussions from a new perspective. For example, the
group reading *Esperanza Rising* (Ryan, 2002) stated their thesis as,
'No matter how hard, never be afraid to start over'. Later, they
asked their classmates to consider the thesis in relation to their
own immigration novels. This presentational talk consolidates the
learning for the presenters and offers new questions/considerations
for the listeners.

Making talk more critical

All the strategies previously described will help to create a classroom
environment in which a culture of talk will thrive. While we were
pleased with the ways our students were using talk, we wanted to create learning environments that encouraged and nurtured critical talk.
On occasions we observed our students engaging in such talk, but we
wanted to understand more about it and to find ways to ensure that
such talk occurred more often. We recognised four important ways in
which we could increase the likelihood that such critical talk would
take place with greater regularity in our classrooms.

Sustaining and strengthening community

While this was not a new strategy for us, we began to reconsider the
significance of a safe environment in which students could explore
shifting world-views that were often unsettling. In addition, society
and the students themselves would exert significant efforts in maintaining the status quo and in discouraging radically new ideas. Our
classroom communities had to become places where sensitive issues
could be discussed; where students could feel comfortable putting
forward an idea one day only to rescind it the next day based on
thoughtful consideration of new information from classmates and
ongoing inquiries; where students could safely challenge one another
for biased or discriminatory words, phrases or actions – and still play
together in the playground or sit together at the lunch table.

Developing new protocols for discussing difficult issues

Talk about highly sensitive issues, particularly those issues that
are emotionally charged for the larger community in which the

classroom functions, is not easy. Just as we had worked to teach students how to talk about literature, we now sought ways to teach students how to talk about difficult issues raised in the literature or in students' worlds outside of school. We therefore developed predictable classroom routines or protocols that could be used for a variety of issues. Many of these protocols were based on the work of those creating democratic classrooms (Fine et al., 1995; Wolk, 1998) and the routines used in peer mediation and non-violent conflict resolution. These protocols have several key components in common.

- Learning to listen closely and with an open mind to the ideas being shared by others.

- Valuing the ideas of all stakeholders and ensuring that all stakeholders have an opportunity to contribute to the process.

- Making a commitment to resolve the conflict or create genuine consensus.

- Setting aside time to reflect on the success or failure of any plans that were developed and implemented.

Working with her primary grade students (6- to 8-year-olds), Kathryn developed a regular classroom structure, which they called the 'Caring Circle'. The Caring Circle was used when the entire class needed to discuss an issue raised by an individual student or a group of students. Common topics were playground disputes, friendship problems, and issues surrounding inclusion/exclusion from a group. In these Caring Circles young students learned to raise issues, consider multiple perspectives, clarify ideas, and explore a variety of potential action plans. They also learned to help others see issues from multiple points of view and to use talk to build support for resolving those issues

Even in Jean's fifth grade, the circle ensured that all ideas, both teachers' and students', were considered and honoured. Jean would push back the chairs and ask students to sit in a circle to debrief playground and behavioural issues. The circle would signal that all opinions were respected. These conversations would then set the stage for any smaller, more independent discussions that students had about challenging books on social topics.

Create a supportive curricular context

Our earlier work with literature discussion groups had convinced us that ideas build over time, becoming more sophisticated as students return to them again and again, with the benefit of new experiences and insights. Both Jean and Kathryn will use text sets to initiate conversations, and to set the stage for reading and discussing a more complex text. When students explore the sets of books and other materials that offer various perspectives on a topic or theme, they will share their prior experiences related to that topic or theme, build up additional background knowledge, raise potential questions, and begin to consider the possibilities for an enquiry to follow.

Kathryn's middle-grade students (11- to 12-year-olds) engaged in conversations about text sets relating to racial discrimination and the Civil Rights Movement, and then connected these to an ongoing look at the phrase 'All men are created equal'. They started by identifying the injustices highlighted by the texts, and then moved onto a critique of this painful period in American history. In the following excerpt, Sam, Jordan, Tom and Colin reflect on how these issues are viewed today compared to how whites and blacks handled such issues in the past.

> **S:** The book I read, *When Marion Sang* (Ryan, 2002), it's about this girl who's really good at singing but she can't sing wherever she wants, like the average white person would be able to do even though she was one of the best singers in the world she wasn't able to. I think it's kinda injustice how back then they couldn't just sing like they want, like whenever they want to in public, that I think ... I like how she, made people, or made people hope that, or she showed people that black people can do the same thing as white people.

> **J:** Yeah that's it, back then but not now, back then it was like even if you were an African American or a Mexican or someone who came from a different country and you were really good at something, like you were a really good lawyer you know a lot about politics, maybe you're good at sports, maybe you're good at all this stuff, but you wouldn't be able to do it because people favour who lives in the country already. Which isn't right because someone, someone could make you a lot of money but you just don't like them so you don't hire them. So it's kinda wrong.

> **T:** I think that, this is just kind of a comment about what we could do based on what Sam said was in that book, I think kind of the perseverance is what keeps prejudice from being really, really bad. Because when you think about it there will probably always be at least one person that's

prejudiced against someone in the way that Jeff said but if as long as there are people that aren't prejudiced and actively trying to be not prejudiced there won't be like, people won't be put back into slavery and everything.

J: Like and it's all about believing that you can still do it. Like Dr Martin Luther King got arrested like 50 times but he always got back out of jail and did the same thing over again. That's why people heard him …

C: Like you said before, people who come to the country, they don't get favoured. I don't understand back in the 1800s through the civil war and slavery, when they were coming over, they said that America was to be the land of tolerance and to honour all peoples' rights but what I don't get is that only white men got rights, nobody else got anything. They were considered inferior and they still kept saying that we are in the right, we get all the equal rights.

J: It's like all about, it's about them just trying to get people to come over because they had so many jobs, need to have people who, it's basically a lie. They say we're the land of tolerance, so if you come over here you'll have rights and lots of money and they come over and they have no choice to go back. So they have to stay and they get taken advantage of.

S: But they kind of had to advertise that or the economy would really fall.

J: But that doesn't mean they had to advertise falsely. Like advertise, isn't that illegal now? To say, advertise something that's wrong? A falsehood?

S: Yeah that's illegal. You could get fined.

J: Well, it wasn't back then.

T: Well this is kind of going back to what I was saying earlier about perseverance and how what you were saying, about Dr Martin Luther King kept on getting arrested yet kept on going. I think that without perseverance you don't really make any difference. Because I mean if you just make one thing that's successful then people think you're good but they won't think you're as good and they won't think that you have as much spirit. (From Wilson, 2004.)

The students identified the injustices related to the Jim Crow laws, and then connected this to their discussion of immigration. They critiqued US immigration practices of bringing in others to support the economy (slaves and low-wage immigrant workers), and then denying these workers the basic rights afforded to 'all men' in the USA. These conversations provided a sturdy foundation for the study of immigration novels that followed. They expanded the themes the students might consider and enriched their under-standing of patterns of discrimination experienced by the charac-ters in their novels.

Highlight cycles of meaning

Our earlier work with literature discussion groups had impressed upon us the way topics re-emerge within a literature discussion of a single title, and across a series of literature discussions of different titles. We knew that when students return to an idea repeatedly, they build up a more sophisticated appreciation for the nuanced mean-ings associated with that idea (Gilles, 1993). Touchstone events can do the same thing for a learning community. Recalling the event, or collection of events, will bring into the conversation all the ques-tions, ideas, and insights explored in the initial discussions. Both teachers take advantage of touchstone events, by reminding stu-dents at appropriate times to recall these experiences.

Kathryn's seventh and eighth grade students were studying civil rights and social action. Part of this enquiry included a full-day visit to the state history museum located nearby. Students looked at paintings of allies attempting to stop a sale of slaves, as well as a small photograph depicting a slave woman holding a toddler entrusted to her care, and protest signs held up in picket lines. They re-enacted a lunch counter sit-in, from both sides of the lunch counter. They handled leg shackles and iron neck collars taken from the nearby courthouse that had been used to restrain and punish slaves. Later, these shackles served as a metaphor for the many ways people try to limit the freedoms of others: words that distinguish between 'us' and 'them', discriminatory laws and practices, and the physical shackles of slavery or jailed inmates. The 'museum visit', and particularly the shackles, became a touchstone event that con-nected the students to one another and allowed them to recall particular conversations in order to make connections to a current discussion topic. At the end of this enquiry, Martha wrote about her new understandings. She drew upon the touchstone event to help her classmates and museum visitors understand her new ideas:

> Shackles are ways that can painfully restrict someone. Stereotypes are like modern day shackles, preventing and judging the person who is being judged.

> We shackle people every day without realising it. Any time you assume, you place a shackle. Sometimes the shackles are invisible but

sometimes they are placed because of physical appearances. Everyone has been shackled whether you know it or not.

Our beliefs about how talk supports learning

The following summarises some of the key beliefs that have emerged from our research and that of others about the role of talking in support of learning. We believe that our classroom environment should be intentionally designed to provide opportunities for students to use:

- *Social talk* – used to bind one to another, and to hold a group or learning community together. When students know and care about one another, differences can become a way of strengthening their combined power to affect and effect change. Students can be inspired to act on behalf of one another, and for others who cannot act or speak for themselves. Students can learn the importance of learning to listen beyond the words to capture the ideas being represented.

- *Exploratory talk* – used to work at understanding new ideas that matter. When students feel comfortable with one another they can begin to explore new boundaries to their learning and to challenge one another's thinking. They can feel safe sharing 'half-baked' ideas, revising their own thinking, and questioning the ideas of others.

- *Presentational talk* – used to share new understandings with others. When students reflect on what they have learned, and consider the audience for their presentations, they can view their learning from a new perspective. Sharing with others can invite students to reflect on their learning.

- *Meta-talk* – used to explore and discuss talk as an artifact. When students make their talk visible, they can become more aware of it and the power it can have to help them think deeply and critically. Jean, especially, helps her students make their talk visible and discuss how their talk and thinking work.

- *Critical talk* – used to invite a critique of students' own views and of contemporary society, the talk of critical conversations. When students engage in critique, they can raise questions about the way things are, dream up possibilities about the way things could be, and then inspire others to join them in making changes.

These forms of talk work interdependently and concurrently in a classroom focused on making and sharing meaning. Each is important for creating meaning, as well as for creating the action to bring about change.

Conclusion

After reading *Dragon's Gate* (Yep, 1995), Jordan said, 'When things change, sometimes you need to change to make them better.' He recognised that not only had the book's characters changed, but also he, as a reader, had changed. We, too, have changed. We have moved from considering how we can use literature and talk to help students understand the text and themselves, to using literature and talk to tackle broad social issues – such as discrimination, equality and justice. In making this journey we have followed the footsteps of many distant teachers. Douglas Barnes's footsteps have been the strongest and most easily followed. His words have kept us moving professionally, have provided us with the tools we needed to look more closely at student talk, and have challenged us to precipitate change. His own body of work has provided us with both the model and the courage to make systemic changes in our work.

References

Bakhtin, M. (1981) *The Dialogic Imagination*. Austin, TX: University of Texas Press.

Barnes, D. (1976) *From Communication to Curriculum*. Harmondsworth: Penguin.

Borden, L. (2002) *America Is ...* New York: Margaret McElderry (Simon & Schuster).

Dickinson, J. (1993) 'Children's perspectives on talk: building a learning community', in K. Pierce and C. Gilles (eds), *Cycles of Meaning: Exploring the Potential of Talk in Learning Communities*. Portsmouth, NH: Heinemann. pp. 99–118.

Fine, E.S., Lacey, A. and Baer, J. (1995) *Children as Peacemakers*. Portsmouth, NH: Heinemann.

Friedman, I. (1987) *How My Parents Learned to Eat*. New York: Houghton Mifflin.

Gilles, C. (1993) '"We make an idea": Cycles of meaning in literature discussion groups', in K. Pierce and C. Gilles (eds), *Cycles of Meaning: Exploring the Potential of Talk in Learning Communities*. Portsmouth, NH: Heinemann. pp. 199–218.

Grossman, M. (photos), Smith, F. (text) (2000) *My Secret Camera: Life in the Lodz Ghetto*. San Diego, CA: Gulliver.

Pierce, K. (2006) 'Recognizing and resisting change: a teacher's professional journey', *Language Arts*, 83 (5): 427–36.

Reeder, C. (1989) *Shades of Gray*. New York: Avon.

Ryan, P. (2002) *Esperanza Rising.* New York: Blue Sky.

Ryan, P. (2002) *When Marian Sang.* New York: Scholastic.

Short, K., Harste, J. with Burke, C. (1988/1996) *Creating Classrooms for Authors and Inquirers.* Portsmouth, NH: Heinemann.

Wilson, J. (2004) 'Talking Beyond the Text: Identifying and Fostering Critical Talking in a Middle School Classroom'. Unpublished dissertation. Missouri: University of Missouri.

Wolk, S. (1998) *A Democratic Classroom.* Portsmouth, NH: Heinemann.

Yep, L. (1995) *Dragon's Gate.* New York: Harpercollins.

The authors wish to thank Jean Dickinson, Jennifer Wilson and Shannon Cuff for their insights and comments throughout the process of writing this chapter.

The Value of Exploratory Talk

Neil Mercer and Lyn Dawes

Summary

In this chapter, the authors argue that teachers and teacher-trainers need a clearer understanding of how talk functions in the classroom, as this will provide the best basis for improving the quality of class-room talk and the educational process more generally. Drawing on their own school-based research and that of others, they show how the concept of 'ground rules' – meaning the normative principles, usually implicit, which govern social behaviour – can be used to examine how talk is actually used by teachers and their students. They then go on to discuss the implications of the findings of this research for ensuring that talk in the classroom is used to good edu-cational effect. Some practical strategies that teachers can use to improve the quality of talk in their classrooms are described.

For Discussion

1 What do Mercer and Dawes mean by saying that most class-room talk is 'asymmetrical'?
2 Can you identify some of the 'ground rules' which underpin the usual pattern of teacher–student interaction in classrooms you have observed?
3 Does it matter that teachers commonly ask a lot of questions?
4 What strategies might a teacher use to modify the ground rules in their classroom, in order to help pupils use talk more actively for learning?
5 What ground rules have been shown to help increase the amount of 'exploratory talk' in a class?

As with other contributors to this book, we have spent a lot of time observing and analysing classroom talk, as well as taking part in it. It is now quite widely appreciated that the quality of classroom dialogue is important for ensuring that children get the most benefit from school, but there still seems to be little progress in improving it. This may be because many teachers, and people involved in teachers' training and development, do not have a clear understanding of how this improvement can be achieved. We offer some relevant information here, drawing on our own research and that of others, including other contributors to this book.

Talk in classrooms is used for many purposes, social as well as educational. Our focus here is on educational talk, meaning the use of spoken language for teaching and learning the curriculum. There is educational talk between pupils and teachers, and educational talk which only involves pupils. Teacher–pupil talk is usually 'asymmetrical', by which we mean one of the participants (usually the teacher) leads the interaction and has the privilege, and responsibility, of being in control. More 'symmetrical' talk, in which partners have a more equal status and potential for control, is likely when groups of pupils work together. Of course classroom talk does not fit neatly into these two categories. Two pupils may not have equal status in a discussion, perhaps because of differences in age or their expertise in a particular subject. In some situations, a pupil may be relatively more expert than a teacher, and this may affect who controls the dialogue. Teachers commonly act as the arbiters of knowledge, using dialogue as a tool for authoritatively demonstrating, explaining, correcting, and so on; but on some occasions they may engage in a more equitable type of dialogue in which a range of views is encouraged and considered. Nevertheless, most talk in classrooms is asymmetrical, with the teacher in the more powerful and authoritative role. As we will explain, this is not necessarily a bad thing. But if learners are to make the best use of talk as a tool for learning, then they need some chance to use it amongst themselves, without a teacher.

From an educational perspective, then, it is vital that both asymmetrical and symmetrical kinds of dialogue happen in classrooms. This point was made, very effectively, by Douglas Barnes in his influential research with Frankie Todd (Barnes and Todd, 1977). But let us consider the quality of talk across both those kinds of circumstances. We know from observational research that in many classrooms most of the talk is not only asymmetrical, it has a particular structure: teachers ask closed questions and children provide brief answers on which the teacher then makes evaluative comments. As we will go on to explain, this represents an unsatisfactory, limited use of the powerful educational tool of language. We also know from classroom research that it is not enough to allow pupils the opportunity for discussion while they carry out educational activities. If simply left to their own devices, their talk is often not productive; some children will be excluded from discussions and the potential value of collaborative learning is squandered. Indeed, we would suggest that the potential power of spoken language is underexploited in most classrooms, in most of the world, most of the time.

Now it may be possible to address this issue by considering, quite separately, what can be done about teacher–pupil talk and what can be done about talk amongst pupils. But we would argue that if we want to achieve the best educational use of talk in a classroom, there needs to be a common underlying approach. So we will discuss each type of talk separately and then try to draw them together. To do so, we will use the concept of 'ground rules' for classroom talk, which came out of research conducted in primary schools in the 1980s (Edwards and Mercer, 1987).

Talk between teachers and pupils

In the 1970s, researchers noticed that talk between a teacher and members of their class was most often organised into a series of three-part exchanges (Sinclair and Coulthard, 1975; Mehan, 1979). First there was an Initiation by the teacher (I) – a question, for example – which stimulated a Response by a child (R) and then some Follow-up or Feedback comment from the teacher (F), which was usually evaluative. The Feedback often initiated another cycle and so the I–R–F pattern was repeated. This type of exchange is still extremely common today, and it is not hard to understand why. Teachers use questions to assess children's understanding, to check their attention, to encourage participation and to provide feedback on what they hear. IRF exchanges are mainly, but not necessarily, associated with closed questions. So how is this pattern of interaction reproduced in classrooms all over the world? It depends on the participants following a set of conversational rules. These 'ground rules' – so called because they are specific to this kind of situation, and are usually left quite implicit – include:

- 'Only a teacher can nominate who should speak.'

- 'Only a teacher may ask a question without seeking permission.'

- 'Only a teacher can evaluate a comment made by a participant.'

- 'Pupils should try to provide answers to teachers' questions which are as relevant and brief as possible.'

- 'Pupils should not speak freely when a teacher asks a question, but should raise their hands and wait to be nominated.'

Pupils who call out an answer without being asked are breaking a rule, and their contribution may thus be treated as 'invisible' until they have been formally asked to speak.

Ground rules for talk are important: they reflect the need for social order of a certain kind to be maintained in classrooms, and the teacher's responsibility for ensuring that any talk and other activity follow an appropriate, curriculum-relevant agenda and trajectory. And classrooms are not peculiar places for having such ground rules; chat shows, job interviews, church services, committee meetings, sales encounters and so on all have their own conversational norms, which participants usually seem to 'pick up' as they are rarely spelt out. The various ground rules which operate in these different types of events will reflect their different functions. Most people take all of this for granted: it seems that this is how social life happens, and will always happen. But the ground rules which have come to operate may not always be the best for pursuing the activity that the participants are trying to get done, and it may help to make these norms explicit and consider if they need to be revised. A new basis for interaction can then be established. In the UK, we have probably all noticed that a change has happened in doctor–patient consultations. The old ground rules used to require patients to simply sit and listen and ask few questions, for doctors to release as little information as possible and to use as technical a language as possible. Nowadays, the talk is usually much more symmetrical and more genuinely communicative. This has not happened naturally, but has required a new focus on communication skills in doctors' initial training and professional development.

Of course, teacher–pupil talk (in the UK) has also not stayed just the same, over the years: it is commonly more informal than was the case a couple of decades ago, and generally speaking the rules do now allow pupils more opportunities to ask questions. But, perhaps surprisingly, the most common type of encounter is still that in which a nominated student provides a brief answer to a question asked by a teacher who already knows the answer. Does this mean that teachers ask too many questions? No, nor does it mean they should avoid IRF exchanges. IRFs can be adapted to serve some varied, useful and interesting purposes (as Wells, 1999, and others have shown). Our own research has found that some teachers who use a lot of questions achieve very good levels of pupil involvement and promote learning (Rojas-Drummond and Mercer, 2004). But they do not only use the traditional, closed types of question, which limit children's involvement with the powerful tool of talk.

We will next present two rather different examples of interactions between a teacher and a student, both happening in the context of a whole-class discussion. In Transcript 1, a Year 7 class are studying acids and alkalis and the teacher has shown them a box of indigestion tablets.

Transcript 1: Indigestion tablets

Teacher: So what do you think the tablets are going to do?

Alex: Um like make them feel better.

Teacher: It's going to make them feel better. Now the question is really how's that happening?

Alex: They're going to neutralise the effect.

Teacher: Ah. You think so? What makes you think that?

Alex: Because the acid, um, the acid in your body.

Teacher: Mmm.

Alex: And there's only so much of it, could there be some form of acid inside the tablets to actually aid the acid [...] to help digest the food?

Teacher: Now – could be, acid add acid – [unintelligible] so that won't neutralise it. So what might it need?

Alex: Alkaline.

Teacher: Ah. Where's the alkali then?

Alex: It could be in the tablets.

This sequence begins with an IRF exchange. We see the teacher's Initiation elicits a Response which is an everyday explanation of the action of the tablets (they make you feel better). The teacher then uses Feedback and a further Initiation to elicit a more scientific kind of explanation. Alex's next Response, that the tablets will 'neutralise the effect', seems not explicit enough for the teacher, who prompts for more information and for a *reason*. Alex's subsequent Response – that there might not be enough acid in the body so the tablets have to top it up – is treated with respect by the teacher, but is also high-lighted as problematic. Alex has introduced the technical term 'neu-tralise', and the teacher is checking for understanding. Asked to think again Alex recalls the word 'alkaline', or perhaps remembers what the word 'neutralise' means; we can't tell, but in either case this is mov-ing towards a more scientific explanation of the action of the tablets. The teacher changes 'alkaline' to 'alkali' in a further Initiation which prompts Alex to suggest that it is in the tablets. Some learning of sci-ence appears to be happening here – and this example shows how a teacher's questions can be used effectively to stimulate and guide pupils' thinking in a productive way.

In Transcript 2, a Year 5 teacher is asking a class to consider the meaning of the prefix 'ex-'. One of the words on the board is 'explode'.

Transcript 2: Explode

Teacher: Explode. EX- is the prefix. Hmm what does explode mean? Hands up. Rory?

Rory: It means it explodes. [*children laugh*]

Teacher: Yes, but, what does explode mean?

Rory: It means, it, explodes! [*children laugh again*]

Teacher: But what does explode mean?

Rory: Say if this pencil exploded, it would go into lots of tiny pieces.

Teacher: Right. It explodes.

These children, who are aged 9 and 10 years, probably all know what 'explode' means. Rory's response to the teacher's Initiation is to appeal to a common, implicit understanding, and the members of the class are amused because they know he has broken a ground rule. In effect, he says to the teacher 'You know what explode means, and we know you know, so I don't need to explain!' The teacher however persists; she needs to know that they do understand the word before they write it down. She may believe that it is of benefit for Rory to articulate a definition of 'explode'; she perhaps wants to be sure that everyone knows what the word means. Eventually Rory comes up with an example, which is accepted. But did any useful learning go on here? It seems unlikely. Dialogue like this can seem unnecessarily long-winded: why didn't the teacher just say, 'explode, meaning to blow up', and save some time? But teachers worry about telling children things they already know – and they worry about what the children don't know. This is one reason why sequences like this are so common. A teacher will want children to become actively involved, which is a good idea, but this may not be the best way to achieve it. The professional skill in using questions lies in knowing why you are using them, and in using different kinds of questions to achieve different ends. While some teachers have a very good intuitive and implicit understanding of this aspect of classroom talk, observational evidence indicates that others don't. Raised awareness of the IRF structure of most classroom talk and guidance in its use could help teachers develop a more effective use of talk, the main tool of their trade.

Another ground rule of talk in most classrooms is that children are expected to respond rapidly to a teacher's question. But is a rapid response always a sensible expectation? Might more thoughtful answers emerge if a pupil is given time to think? An interesting variant of the IRF exchange was first described by our research colleague Rupert Wegerif, who noted that some pupils working at computers would stop at decision points (Initiation), turn away from the screen, and talk about what to do (Discussion) before carrying on (Response) (as described in Wegerif and Dawes, 2004). The incidence of IDRF was higher among pupils whose teachers encouraged discussion; and its use was shown to be productive in terms of thinking and learning. It seemed that children felt they were able to do this because they knew that the computer, unlike a teacher, is infinitely patient. But teachers can also create opportunities for pupils to discuss before they respond. We recorded talk in a Year 1 class in which a teacher had introduced the topic of the distinction between living and non-living things. Through a whole-class discussion, the teacher had found that some children were surprised by the idea that plants are alive. Following up on this new interest, the teacher asked (I), 'Why do you think trees have leaves?' and requested the pupils to think together with a partner (D) before responding. After five minutes' discussion, the children suggested these ideas:

Why do trees have leaves?

For food or shelter for animals.

To catch rain.

So we know when it's autumn.

To make the wind.

To look nice.

For camouflage.

For decoration.

Such responses provided the teacher with a clearer idea about what the children thought. This mix of magic, imagination and pragmatic deduction became the starting point for further work in which pupils learned about the lives of plants. A Discussion element allows pupils to reveal their thinking in a safe forum before presenting them in public. The teacher's professional expertise in the use of IDRF lies in asking genuine, stimulating, Initiation questions; and in generating in the class the common understanding that discussion is what we do to learn in school.

In Chapter 2 of this book, Phil Scott provides a scheme for distinguishing ways that teachers can interact with pupils, and considers the function and value of each of these 'communicative approaches' (Mortimer and Scott, 2003). He characterises an interaction between teacher and pupils as being either *interactive* or *non-interactive*, and either *dialogic* or *authoritative*. Transcript 3 is an example of a sequence which is, in Scott's terms dialogic/interactive. A Year 6 class, studying electricity, were about to wrap iron nails with wire and attach a battery to see if they could make an electromagnet. The teacher has shown the class two types of nails, large and small.

Transcript 3: Magnetic nails

Teacher: There's two different nails here; what do you reckon, do you think the big ones will work better or the little ones?

Class: Big ones.

Teacher:	Now is that a guess or have you got a good reason for saying that? Floella?
Floella:	A guess.
Teacher:	A guess.
William:	I've got a reason.
Teacher:	You've got a reason?
William:	Well I think that the big one will become a magnet, because it's bigger – and actually no, I've changed my mind, it's the little one because the little one is smaller and the more, more um electricity can go around it, because if it's the big one it will only pick up a little bit.
Teacher:	So we, there's two reasons there, and arguing both cases isn't there? Yes Sam?
Sam:	Um I think the little one will work better because it'll be less, the energy running through it to make it a magnet will be less dispersed than in the big one, because there's more *things* to make a magnet.
Teacher:	More things to make a magnet? More current per?
Sam:	More iron to make into a magnet.
Teacher:	More current per amount of iron?
Sam:	Yeah so you'd need a bigger current.
Teacher:	Right, well let's give it a go shall we?

The teacher has no idea which nail will be a stronger magnet, and asks a genuine question. The pupils offer a guess (possibly thinking, bigger is going to be stronger) then some reasoned ideas. We can see that there is some thinking going on. The ideas are half-formed; pupils are airing their thoughts in an open, inquisitive way to collaborate in solving the problem. Sam's idea – that the energy running through the smaller nail will be 'less dispersed' and that the bigger nail has more *things* in it that would need to be magnetised – is quite sophisticated and reflects a personal interest in all things scientific. This understanding – which is testable therefore a good scientific hypothesis – is brought out by this dialogue for the class's benefit.

We have identified some strategies that can be used to engage pupils in productive, extended dialogues in whole-class sessions. But we must stress the importance of *context* for making any strategy effective. For example, the question 'Why do you think that?' asked by two differ-ent teachers on the same topic may generate quite different types of responses from their classes, because one teacher has established a classroom in which pupils know that the ground rules allow and encourage extended responses and tentative, exploratory contribu-tions, while the other teacher has not. Strategies are only likely to be effective when a suitable context of shared understanding has been established. Once that has been done, our observations suggest that the following strategies can be useful.

- Make it clear that some parts of lessons are expressly intended to be discussion sessions, in which questions and diverse views on a topic can be expressed.

- During whole-class discussions, allow a series of responses to be made without making any immediate evaluations.

- If some different views have been expressed, ask pupils for the reasons and justifications for their views before proceeding.

- Precede whole-class discussion of particular questions or issues with a short group-based session, in which pupils can prepare joint responses for sharing with the class. It may help to offer pupils a set of alternative explanations, contentious statements or ideas on a topic, and to ask them to decide which are true/false, and why.

- Before providing a definitive account or explanation (of, for example, a scientific phenomenon) elicit several children's current ideas on the topic. Then link your explanation to these ideas.

- Use whole-class sessions to gather feedback from children about how they have worked together in groups. Are the ground rules working? Do the rules need to be revised? Do they feel their discussions have been constructive? If not, why not? And what could be done about it?

- Ask pupils to nominate other pupils in whole-class discussions, so that the teacher does not always get to choose who should speak.

So one way that the quality of talk in a classroom can be improved is for a teacher to become more aware of how they talk with chil-dren, and then to review and redesign their own use of talk. But in itself that would not be enough: consideration also needs to be given to developing the talk repertoires of pupils.

Talk amongst pupils

Amongst pupils, as we explained earlier, talk is usually more symmetrical. That means that different ground rules operate. For example, it is usually acceptable for anyone to ask a question, to interrupt a speaker and to disagree with an opinion. People don't have to wait to be nominated to speak, and they may often take quite long turns. Digressions into topics other than the educational task in hand are also usually considered more acceptable than in teacher–student talk. But are the ground rules that usually operate sufficient and adequate enough to ensure that useful, productive talk is usually generated? The answer provided by observational research is 'no'. In our own early research, we went looking for productive talk amongst children in classrooms – and found very little (Wegerif and Scrimshaw, 1997). The reasons, we concluded, were connected to the implicit, almost invisible nature of conversational ground rules. Many children either don't know how to carry on a productive discussion, or don't realise that this is what they are expected to do by their teacher. On the other hand, teachers can assume (wrongly) that children do know how to make productive discussion happen. The nature of 'productive discussion', in the special context of group-based educational activity in school, is not normally something that teachers and pupils discuss, so they go about classroom life without the benefit of a shared understanding of this important aspect of how to make it happen successfully.

In his chapter in this book, Douglas Barnes describes an educationally important type of talk between pupils who are working together as 'exploratory talk':

> Exploratory talk is hesitant and incomplete because it enables the speaker to try out ideas, to hear how they sound, to see what others make of them, to arrange information and ideas into different patterns ... [In] presentational talk the speaker's attention is primarily focussed on adjusting language, content and manner to the needs of an audience, and in exploratory talk the speaker is more concerned with sorting out his or her own thoughts. (Barnes, this volume, p. 5)

In exploratory talk, then, a speaker 'thinks aloud', taking the risk that others can hear, and comment on, partly-formed ideas. Engaging in exploratory talk is therefore rather a brave thing to do, and tends not to happen unless there is a degree of trust within a discussion group. From Barnes's definition, exploratory talk might be seen as a kind of lone venture for the individual. Its potentially rich benefits stem from the way that thinking aloud precipitates ideas, as the mind draws on previously unconnected reserves to come up with something new, creative, or well-reasoned. Barnes's achievement in this definition was to help teachers see that learning happens through talk between pupils working in groups, and not just through the talk between teachers and pupils, and that a certain, rather adventurous kind of talk might require a symmetrical (and teacher-free) dialogic context.

Working with several colleagues we have continued this search and, in the process, have extended the concept of exploratory talk to cover not only its function for the individual speaker, but for the work of the group of which they are part. We were influenced here by the Russian psychologist Vygotsky's (1978) proposal that language is not only a psychological tool for individuals to use to 'try out ideas', but is also a cultural tool whereby people can use language to 'think together'. In exploratory talk, listeners gain the benefit of hearing a speaker's tentative thoughts. Feedback from listeners may require a speaker to elaborate their point of view, to perhaps cast it in a clearer, more persuasive form – or even to change their mind. Talk of an exploratory kind is thus not only useful for an individual to sort out their thoughts, it can also help two or more people to solve problems because they are sharing ideas (some of which may only be partly developed) in a genuinely collaborative interaction. A situation can be created wherein the tentative expression and evaluation of ideas are collective enterprises. For this to happen, there must not only be a sense of trust and common endeavour, but also a shared understanding of how to engage in a productive discussion. From this more dialogic perspective, we decided that the ground rules which enable exploratory talk should include the following:

- Partners engage critically but constructively with each other's ideas.

- Everyone participates.

- Tentative ideas are treated with respect.

- Ideas offered for joint consideration may be challenged.

- Challenges are justified and alternative ideas or understandings are offered.

- Opinions are sought and considered before decisions are jointly made.

- Knowledge is made publicly accountable (and so reasoning is visible in the talk).

We deduced that in order for such educationally effective talk to happen more often, pupils and teachers needed to be more aware of how it could be made to happen. This would mean them examining the ground rules which they currently used, and if necessary revising them to be more like those set out for exploratory talk. With our colleagues, we therefore devised an approach to developing classroom discussion, supported by curriculum-related activities, which we called *Thinking Together*. To cut a long story short, the research which we then pursued for a decade supported this hypothesis. We found that raising awareness of the importance of exploratory talk, and teaching pupils exactly how to make it happen, did increase the incidence of exploratory talk, helping both primary and secondary children to learn successfully through discussion-based activities (Mercer and Littleton, 2007).

The children in Transcript 4, below, were members of a Year 5 class in which the teacher had used the Thinking Together approach and so had established with the class some ground rules for how they would talk in groups (which roughly corresponded to those we set out earlier for exploratory talk). The sequence was recorded during a lesson on 'the Earth in space' in which the teacher had set up the kind of IDRF activity we described earlier. As a group of three, they had been asked to discuss the statement *'The moon shines because it is alight'* and decide whether it was true, false, or if they were unsure about which it might be.

Transcript 4: The moon shines

Lara: [*reading*] The moon shines because it's alight.

Celia: Alight … ?

Gemma: Um, I think yeah, it is alight but um, it doesn't exactly shine.

Lara: Shine.

Gemma: It doesn't shine that much, it is, it's like it is really really bright white.

Lara: Like a bright white.

Gemma: 'Cos it's really dark at night.

Lara: Yes.

Gemma: So it brights up, cos, once there was a full moon, every time that there's a full moon for some reason you can see a smiley face on, on the moon and when you see that smiley face on the moon, you can see, you can see this um, you can see light around it and it's, and it shines really brightly and ...

Lara: Ah, I know what you mean there.

Gemma: Yes, and it doesn't mean that it's alight, it's just really shiny, really bright white.

Lara: OK, so what shall we say?

Celia: I think we should do ... true.

Lara: I'm not, I'm not really sure that it is, um, why don't we say unsure?

Gemma: Yes, 'cos I mean, it is a bright white moon, it, it's not alight.

Lara: Yes.

Gemma: It hasn't got a light bulb in it has it?

This is not talk that leads to a scientifically accurate solution. The group are struggling at the limits of their knowledge. And their ground rules are not strictly maintained. Celia is not asked for her ideas and does not participate very fully in this discussion. But the talk has some 'exploratory' features: the participants are sticking to the task in hand; they act as if they respect one another; they offer ideas with reasons (note the three uses of "cos'); they try out tentative thoughts using 'but ...'. Gemma, in particular, attempts to summon up some relevant information. They accept one another's changes of mind and readily admit that they don't know. Gemma moves from thinking the moon might be alight to saying that it isn't. Much talk of an exploratory kind in classrooms is like this example: imperfect in terms of the reasoning and generating knowledge, but still valuable in terms of harnessing social learning to promote thinking and motivation. Linked through the IDRF activity to a subsequent whole-class discussion, it can help pupils consider what they know and don't know, and may help teachers see what might be the next most useful steps to pursue on the basis of children's current state of understanding.

To our rules for exploratory talk we might add 'Ideas are elaborated when necessary, so that everyone understands what is meant.' But this requirement is not necessarily obvious to children involved in a discussion. Elaboration requires thinking on the part of a speaker, puts more evidence for decision making forward, and can promote social cohesion in a group by helping pupils understand one another's point of view. Douglas Barnes said 'If it can be shown that groups can *learn* to elaborate, this would be an important educational finding'(1992: 66). Our research has shown that teachers can indeed help children develop this useful communicative skill and we have described some ways that they can do so (Dawes, 2008).

Creating dialogic classrooms

Having considered teacher–pupil talk and talk amongst pupils, we next want to consider how these can be brought together within one framework. We can draw here on the work of other contributors to this book. In Chapter 10, Gordon Wells and Tamara Bell explain how teachers can make their classrooms *communities of inquiry* where they lead, help, and join in with pupils' learning through dialogue. In such classrooms, there is a balance between teacher-led discussion and talk in which pupils exercise more control, with the dialogue as a whole being linked through joint processes of investigation and problem solving. This involves the generation of a more dialogic form of teaching-and-learning than is usually found in schools. Robin Alexander (2006) has also argued the need for a new pedagogy. As he explains in Chapter 6, *dialogic teaching* can harness the power of talk to engage children, stimulate and extend their thinking, and advance their understanding. It involves teachers developing their own awareness and skill in using talk, and helping their pupils to develop their own awareness and communicative effectiveness, namely, that the achievement of classroom education of a 'dialogic' kind must include, somewhere in the cumulative process of joint knowledge-building, some training for both teachers and pupils in how to use talk to best effect for pursuing educational activities. From our own work with teachers, we have also concluded that a new, more dialogic approach is required, in which talk is used effectively as a tool for joint enquiry. This requires the development of a more reflective, critical appreciation of how that tool can be used by both teachers and children.

Conclusion

Research has shown that simply putting children into groups and leaving them to solve problems by themselves is not enough to ensure that they will use cooperation and dialogue to good effect. Yet research has also confirmed Douglas Barnes's early conviction that talk amongst pupils can make an important contribution to their learning. There is no paradox here, once it has been appreciated that whole-class, teacher-led discussion and group-based activities are not alternative ways of learning, but complementary ones. Children need a careful combination of teacher guidance (through whole-class, teacher-led activities) and group work (in which they can try out ways of using language to solve problems together). For some children, school may provide their only real opportunity for learning how to engage in focussed, reasoned discussion and so develop important language and thinking skills. It is important for teachers to provide such opportunities, in three main ways.

First, they should *take an active role, guiding their pupils' use of language and modelling the ways it can be used for thinking collectively*. Partly, this is a matter of the teacher practising what they preach. If a teacher wants children to ask for reasons and provide them, then that teacher should do so themselves in whole-class discussions. If, in group discussions, pupils are expected to treat tentative ideas with respect, to ensure that different points of view are heard and to elaborate ideas so that everyone understands them, the teacher must do likewise when talking with the class. They should ask children to give reasons to support their views, engage them in extended discussions of topics, and encourage them to see that responding need not simply mean providing the 'right answer'. Plenary sessions can be used to help children reflect on their activities and consolidate their learning about language use.

Second, teachers should *establish an appropriate set of ground rules for talk in class*, building on children's own raised awareness of how language can be used. These rules then become part of the common knowledge of the class. Early on in this chapter we noted the differences between teacher–pupil talk and talk amongst pupils, using the concept of symmetry/asymmetry. Some different ground rules will, and must, operate in those different settings. But if the potential value of dialogue for teaching and learning is to be realised, all the talk in class must be underpinned by some common principles and, hence, some common ground rules.

Third, a teacher needs to ensure that *group activities are well designed to elicit debate and joint reasoning*. The concept of a 'community of inquiry' is relevant here. Good activities are those which require a careful, reasoned consideration of different ways of solving problems, or the evaluation of different, possible explanations in tasks that are meaningful to children. Activities should draw on children's existing common knowledge, but should also draw them beyond it into a consideration of new ideas and the search for more useful information. Examples of these kinds of activities, in practical, tried and tested forms, are set out in our books for teachers (Dawes et al., 2003; Dawes and Sams, 2004; Dawes, 2008), but it is perfectly possible for teachers to devise their own.

References

Alexander, R. (2006) *Towards Dialogic Teaching*. York: Dialogos.

Barnes, D. (1976) *From Communication to Curriculum*. Harmondsworth: Penguin.

Barnes, D. (1992) *From Communication to Curriculum* (second edition). Portsmouth, NH: Boynton/Cook.

Barnes, D. and Todd, F. (1977) *Communication and Learning in Small Groups*. Abingdon: Routledge and Kegan Paul.

Dawes, L. (2008) *The Essential Speaking and Listening: Talk For Learning at KS2*. Abingdon: Routledge.

Dawes, L., Mercer, N. and Wegerif, R. (2003) *Thinking Together: A Programme of Activities for Developing Speaking, Listening and Thinking Skills for Children Aged 8–11*. Birmingham: Imaginative Minds.

Dawes, L. and Sams, C. (2004) *Talk Box: Speaking and Listening Activities for Learning at Key Stage 1*. London: David Fulton.

Edwards, D. and Mercer, N. (1987) *Common Knowledge: The Development of Understanding in the Classroom*. Abingdon: Routledge.

Mehan, H. (1979) *Learning Lessons: Social Organization in the Classroom*. Cambridge, MA: Harvard University Press.

Mercer, N. and Littleton, K. (2007) *Dialogue and the Development of Children's Thinking: A Sociocultural Approach*. Abingdon: Routledge.

Mortimer, E.F. and Scott, P.H. (2003) *Meaning Making in Science Classrooms*. Buckingham: Open University Press.

Rojas-Drummond, S. and Mercer, N. (2004) 'Scaffolding the development of effective collaboration and learning', *International Journal of Educational Research*, 39: 99–111.

Sinclair, J. and Coulthard, R. (1975) *Towards An Analysis of Discourse: The English Used by Teachers and Pupils*. Oxford: Oxford University Press.

Vygotsky, L.S. (1978) *Mind in Society: The Development of Higher Psychological Processes*. Cambridge, MA: Harvard University Press.

Wegerif, R. and P. Scrimshaw (eds) (1997) *Computers and Talk in the Primary Classroom*. Clevedon: Multilingual Matters.

Wegerif, R. and Dawes, L. (2004) *Thinking and Learning with ICT*. Abingdon: Routledge/Falmer.

Wells, G. (1999). *Dialogic Inquiry: Toward A Sociocultural Practice And Theory Of Education*. Cambridge: Cambridge University Press.

5

Talking to Learn and Learning to Talk in the Mathematics Classroom

Yvette Solomon and Laura Black

Summary

This chapter is concerned with how talk is used in mathematics education. The authors explain how students can adopt different 'learner identities' and different ways of participating in classroom dialogue, and argue that these different forms of interaction can be important influences on students' engagement with, and learning of, mathematics. Drawing on observation in a primary school classroom and interviews with secondary/high school students, they argue that talk should be considered as a means for both providing a teacher's expert guidance and for enabling students to take ownership of their learning of mathematics. The authors conclude that, to be most effective, mathematics education needs a pedagogy which explicitly encourages the active engagement of students in dialogue, and that mathematics teachers need to critically review their current practice accordingly.

For Discussion

1 What do Solomon and Black mean by 'identities of engagement' and 'identities of exclusion', and how do they relate to your own experiences of learning and/or teaching mathematics?
2 What are some possible reasons why a traditional 'chalk-and-talk' approach has tended to persist in mathematics teaching?

(Continued)

(Continued)

3   What pedagogic strategies do the authors propose for changing students' roles as learners of mathematics?

4   What evidence is offered that the use of different dialogic strategies increases students' engagement with the subject?

One of the distinctive and perhaps under-emphasised elements of Douglas Barnes's work is his recognition that pupils do not necessarily participate in classroom talk in the same way: instead, their contributions to classroom talk, and the type of talk directed towards them by the teacher, vary from pupil to pupil. Barnes (1976) was keen to move away from explanations, current at the time, which suggested that the educational failure of some children was an inevitable consequence of their social and linguistic backgrounds. Instead, he argued that given the right context in terms of task and pedagogic approach all children are capable of good quality exploratory talk – that is, talk which involves the learner in 're-arranging their thoughts during improvised talk' (1976: 108). This kind of talk is a means of taking an active part in learning in that the learner uses language to 'shape knowledge for themselves' with a corresponding hallmark characteristic of tentativeness, 'accompanying (and displaying) the detours and dead-ends of thinking' (p. 108).

Thirty years on this argument is still highly relevant, and particularly so in the context of school mathematics. In this chapter, we show how pupils take on different learner identities and ways of engaging with knowledge through their participation and non-participation in classroom discourse. While some students readily develop an identity of engagement which involves hypothesising and posing questions for oneself, exploring and connecting ideas, negotiating and justifying solutions to problems and using the teacher as a resource, others will develop an identity of exclusion from mathematics. Like Barnes, we see the source of these differences in the interaction patterns that pupils experience; dialogic interactions enable some pupils to 'talk themselves into understanding', whereas heavily controlled interactions enforce a passive role. It can also be argued that the strong emphasis on ability and attainment in the current UK climate impacts on teachers' communicative behaviour and, consequently, on students' understanding of the learning process (Reay and Wiliam, 1999; Myhill, 2002; Black, 2004b; 2007; Solomon, 2007; 2008. We conclude that the processes involved in the construction of identities of exclusion from mathematics begin early in the school career. Such processes will continue to occur so long as the emphasis on a performance agenda remains the bedrock of educational policy.

Agency in the learning process

In Chapter 1 of this volume, Douglas Barnes introduces the idea of 'working on understanding', going on to identify this as '"trying out" new ways of thinking and understanding some aspect of the world: the trying out enables us to see how far a new idea will take us, what it will or will not explain, where it contradicts our other beliefs, and where it opens up new possibilities' (this volume, page 5). This crucial aspect of constructing understanding is central to our analysis of learning mathematics in this chapter. We focus in particular on the role of the teacher in providing a context for learning through talk, mindful of Barnes's comment that 'the ability to think aloud and to share thoughts with others is not universal, and is not necessarily linked to academic intelligence. Some young people need help to develop these skills and even to discover what *discussion* is' (this volume, pages 7–8). We are concerned to underline not only the need for talk in mathematics learning, but also the possibility that not all learners are given the opportunity to engage with it.

In order to 'try out' new ways of thinking, we need to perceive ourselves as having some agency in or control over what we are doing. As long ago as 1976, Barnes identified a 'performance climate' in many classrooms (1976: 111) which detracted from such agency, creating a dynamic which disempowers pupils and prevents them from reflecting on their own thinking and pre-existing knowledge in order to relate new to old. The loss of collaboration with teachers in negotiating learning causes pupils to look only for the answer that a teacher wants: 'When a teacher *assesses* what his pupils say he distances himself from their views, and allies himself with external standards which may implicitly devalue what the learner himself has constructed' (1976: 111). In contrast, 'when a teacher *replies* to his pupils, he is by implication taking their view of the subject seriously, even though he may wish to extend and modify it' (1976: 111): such interactions attribute a higher status to the learners' contributions, underlining their ownership of the learning that is going on. It is the dialogic quality of such interactions – questioning to invite surmise and the reorganisation of ideas, and (most importantly) collaborative discussion which picks up what is said and extends, modifies or even challenges it – that enables genuine construction of knowledge.

Fostering agency through talk in mathematics education

> Mathematics is associated with certainty, and with being able to give quickly the correct answer; doing mathematics corresponds to following rules prescribed by the teacher; knowing mathematics means being able to recall and use the correct rule when asked by the teacher; and an answer to a mathematical question or problem becomes true when it is approved by the authority of the teacher (de Corte et al., 2002: 305).

Perhaps more than any other school subject, mathematics has suffered from the 'talk-and-chalk' approach associated with entrenched assumptions on the part of both teachers and learners regarding ability and the nature of the subject. It is highly likely to be taught in ability groups (Ireson and Hallam, 2001), where ability itself is defined in terms of speed and a perception that 'you can either do it or you can't', with the ultimate hallmark of 'being good at maths' in England and Wales being membership of the elite group which takes the compulsory General Certificate of Secondary Education (GCSE) examination up to a year earlier than the majority of school pupils (Boaler, 1997; Boaler et al., 2000). As Schoenfeld (1992: 359) says, the common perception which sustains and is sustained by traditional teaching is that:

> Mathematics problems have one and only one right answer.
>
> There is only one correct way to solve any mathematics problem – usually the rule the teacher has most recently demonstrated to the class.
>
> Mathematics is a solitary activity, done by individuals in isolation.

In order to counter these assumptions, mathematics education reform has sought to 'promote meaningful learning' (Nathan and Knuth, 2003: 175) by creating opportunities for exploratory talk. Building on broadly constructivist approaches, critics of traditional mathematics teaching emphasise the role of the classroom community in supporting students' learning via conjecture, experiment, argument and justification (Cobb et al., 1993; Bauersfeld, 1995; Williams and Baxter, 1996; Martino and Maher, 1999; NCTM, 2000; Maher, 2005). Recent UK education policy has adopted this philosophy, exhorting teachers 'to encourage a more active approach towards learning Mathematics and to develop more connected and challenging teaching methods' (DfES, 2005: 5). This approach brings with it an emphasis on the role of classroom interaction in learning and the teacher's role in it as 'eliciting and engaging children's thinking; listening carefully; monitoring classroom conversations and deciding when to step in and when to step aside' (Nathan and Knuth, 2003: 176). The classroom community can support this process through the collective production and maintenance of social norms and relationships (Michaels et al., 2002) which ensure that ideas are respected, listened to and extended by both teachers and other pupils in a 'community of enquiry' (Mercer and Fisher, 1998) or 'interthinking' (Mercer, 2000).

As Douglas Barnes's analysis of classroom interaction shows, support- ing 'meaningful learning' is a question of fostering discussion between pupils, enabling exploration and exploratory talk (which includes chal- lenge and justification), and assisting learners to connect ideas and for- mulate them in a mathematical but critical way (Barnes and Sheeran, 1992). Such connections rely on a teacher's ability to establish a joint frame of reference (Edwards and Mercer, 1987) with their pupils and to build on it, making use of the physical context of material props and relevant shared prior knowledge, and appropriating, modifying and feeding back pupils' ideas. However, as Edwards and Mercer also demonstrated, the power imbalance between teachers and pupils and the pressure of school performance measures mean that shared frames of reference are frequently sacrificed as discussion is abandoned or quashed and opportunities for appropriating prior pupil knowledge are missed. Thus pupils frequently guess what teachers want them to say in pursuit of providing them with 'final draft' answers, rather than reflecting upon their own ideas and genuinely engaging with the teacher's expertise. Edwards and Mercer (1987) suggest that the former may result in the acquisition of ritual knowledge, understanding which is 'embedded in the paraphernalia of the lesson' (1987: 99) rather than an understanding of the key principles. It appears that mathematics becomes particularly vulnerable because, as Douglas Barnes points out earlier in this book, ' ... the way teachers interact with their pupils is closely linked to their preconceptions about the nature of the knowl- edge that they are teaching. If they see their role as simply the trans- mission of authoritative knowledge they are less likely to give their pupils the opportunity to explore new ideas' (this volume, page 8). So, despite the research and the policy aims, the emphasis on performance and on mathematics as certain knowledge dominates classroom interaction, and indeed OFSTED (2006: 2–3) reported on the prevalence of 'Teaching which presents mathematics as a collection of arbitrary rules and procedures, allied to a narrow range of learning activities in lessons which do not engage students in real mathematical thinking'. In the following sections we show how the current climate of education consequently engenders the development of agency in mathematics for only some pupils, leaving others marginalised and disempowered.

The development of learner identities in primary school

In this section we present data from an ethnographic study of a Year 5 (aged 9 to 10 years) mathematics classroom which demonstrate patterns of differential participation in whole-class discussions. The study highlighted that while some students were willing contributors who consistently engaged in exploratory talk, others regularly experienced heavily controlled question and answer sessions where their input was limited to passive, monosyllabic answers (see Black, 2004a, 2004b, for more details). Our intention here is to show how experiencing these contrasting forms of teacher–pupil interaction shapes pupils' opportunities to develop an understanding of mathematics and the application of mathematical concepts and methods and, in so doing, asserts agency over their learning.

The first example occurred in a lesson in which pupils had to calculate how many sets of nine skittles can be made from any given quantity. Here, the teacher (T) is encouraging pupils to use a short cut when calculating the answer by utilising a well-known finger trick.

> **T:** Right who does know what I'm talking about? [*Phillip puts his hand up*] Go on then Phillip.
>
> **Phillip:** You put ten. [*He holds both hands up with palms facing the class*]
>
> **T:** Right you put your hands up like this … you're better off if you do it that way round, aren't you? [*Phillip turns his hands round so his palms face inwards*]
>
> **Phillip:** Then you take one away like that [*putting one finger down*] and then you go …
>
> **T:** So for three nines what would you do then? Show me what you do with your fingers. Hold your hands in front of you like that.

Phillip: [*Holding hands up*] You got well one times nine is …

T: One times nine is the first finger. So you put that one down and what you've got left is …? Nine. Then nine is nine and then …

Phillip: … Add ten equals nineteen take away the one for two …

T: Ooh is that the way you do it?

Phillip: And then you go … then add ten is twenty-eight and take away one is twenty-seven …

T: Twenty-seven. Aaah that's brilliant Phillip, do you know I didn't know that one.

In this interaction, the teacher gives Phillip, a regular contributor to class discussions, the opportunity to hold the floor and carry out a successful 'public' demonstration of his own version of the 'finger trick'. She uses prompts to encourage Phillip to explain his thinking more clearly (that is, by using his hands more visibly, 'Hold your hands in front of you like that') for the benefit of the other pupils. In response, Phillip engages in a form of talk which is driven by the need to clearly describe his method to a given audience. He builds on the teacher's reformulations as the interaction progresses, efficiently moving on to the next stage of the trick once his previous input has been modified by the teacher. As Barnes (1976: 41) has argued, having the opportunity to explain their thinking in this way enables learners to take ownership of their knowledge: ' … the shaping of language is a means by which pupils reach a deeper understanding of what they have already partly grasped'.

Furthermore, this interaction reveals Phillip's self-confidence in himself as a learner – he is not deterred by the teacher's recognition that his version was not the method she had in mind ('Ooh is that the way you do it?'). This is perhaps a result of her use of 'reply' type responses which, as we have noted above, assign a higher status to the learner's contributions/ideas. Consequently, he is able to establish his own version of the finger trick as a legitimate contribution to the knowledge under discussion. Particularly significant is the teacher's final comment 'Aah that's brilliant Phillip, do you know I didn't know that one …' which publicly recognises his expertise. Thus, not only is Phillip given space to present his own ideas by the teacher, he has also learnt to actively embrace such opportunities by contributing his own knowledge/experience: he has agency as a mathematics learner.

However, this kind of dialogue was not experienced by all students in this classroom. The following interaction involved Janet, who had recently joined the class half-way through the academic year. She was born in China but had lived in another big city in the north-west of England for two years. In this lesson the children are working on a textbook task on fractions, using an egg-box to represent the whole number; they have to calculate the number of eggs which represent a given fraction.

> **T:** Eh number six, what is four sixths of four ... of ... what's four-sixths of six eggs? So what's the first thing to do ... we do Janet? To find out four-sixths of six eggs. Got to find out ...
>
> **Janet:** Four.
>
> **T:** Not four, the bottom number remember is telling you how many parts you're dividing it in to, so which number do you share it by? [*Other pupils have hands up*]
>
> **P2:** Six.
>
> **T:** Six yeh it's the six underneath, it's the bottom part of the fraction isn't it? That's telling you how many parts you're sharing, whatever the number is, whether it's a hundred or twenty, a two, a six or eight or one thousand five hundred and sixty five, it's still being shared between that ... into that number of equal groups is it not? [*Teacher is animated with hands here*]
>
> **Janet:** Yeh [*quietly*].
>
> **T:** Yeh, so you're sharing it by six, how many sixes are in six? ... [*pause*] ... one. So you'd have one, yeh, so what would four sixths be then?
>
> **Janet:** Four.
>
> **T:** Four ... yeh ... is that what you were telling me before? Was it the answer you were giving me? I'm sorry [*sympathetically*].

This extended bout of teacher questioning is reminiscent of what Edwards and Mercer (1987) describe as 'cued elicitation', in which a teacher tries to shape a pupil's input through continued questions with a pre-determined answer in mind. Here we see this in action; the teacher mishears Janet's correct answer because she is committed to eliciting a specific kind of response (namely, the method of calculation – 'So what's the first thing to do ... we do Janet?'). Janet is forced into a passive, monosyllabic role in which she has to focus on working through the teacher's agenda regardless of her understanding. Not surprisingly, she appears to become confused and fails to respond to the teacher's further question ('Which number do you share it by?'). Her remaining input is then limited to a tentative agreement with the teacher regarding the correctness of her explanation ('yeh') and a repetition of her original answer ('four'). In contrast to Phillip, Janet's attempt to provide a legitimate contribution to the discussion is interpreted as inappropriate (or incorrect) and consequently she is given little space to use the interaction and the linguistic tools of school mathematics to jointly construct ideas with the teacher and other pupils in the class.

However, Janet had not always occupied this passive role during her time in Class 5W. The following interaction was recorded in an earlier lesson on fractions, where the task involved working out what fraction of a number of eggcups contained an egg:

Janet:	Do you only count the eggs that are in the eggcups?
T:	What?
Janet:	Do you only count ...
T:	Ooh no because altogether you've got six. How many have you got?
T and Janet:	Five.
T:	So that's the whole ... is five. So each one of those is a fifth. And how many out of five are in the eggcups?
Janet:	Three.
T:	Three out of the five.
Janet:	So that's three ...
T:	Three fifths.

Here we see Janet attempt to use the teacher as a resource in order to clarify her understanding of the task ('Do you only count the eggs that are in the eggcups?'). The teacher's initial response is to clarify Janet's question ('What?'), but once again it appears that she misunderstands. She instructs her not to count the eggs in the eggcups and proceeds to model the calculation ('So that's the **whole** ... is five. So each one of those is a **fifth**.'). But then she asks 'And how many out of five are in the eggcups?' which suggests that Janet should indeed count the eggs in the eggcups. Despite this potential confusion, Janet remains engaged in the interaction throughout and not only answers the teacher's questions when prompted but also seeks to clarify the meaning she has drawn from the modelling process ('So that's three … ?'). The outcome of this interaction is that Janet clarifys that her strategy for calculating a fraction of a whole number (namely, counting the eggs in the cups) is correct, and the teacher has modelled some mathematical terminology ('three fifths').

A comparison of these last two interactions highlights how the pupil's role can vary and change in the classroom over time. In this second (earlier) interaction, Janet exerts some sense of control over her learning by seeking the teacher's help in clarifying her understanding of fractions. This was not apparent in the episode of 'cued elicitation' which took place at a later date, and was symptomatic of a general change in Janet's positioning as a mathematical learner. The motivation behind this change is not clear, but it may be associated with the teacher's preconceptions of Janet's mathematical competencies and her resulting behaviour within such interactions. In a later interview the teacher observed that 'certain things appeared to floor' Janet. It may be that Janet's repeated attempts to understand what she was doing with fractions (as seen in the earlier interaction) suggested to the teacher that she was struggling to get to grips with the topic, informing her expectations regarding Janet's level of ability and what could be expected from her when interacting in whole-class discussions.

As the year progressed, Janet participated in class discussions less and less, moving from a position in which she had access to interactions which resulted in a clarification/development of her understanding to one in which she was inclined to guess what answer the teacher wanted through a limited level of participation. Eventually, her participation in interactions with the teacher became somewhat limited and she made very few contributions to whole-class discussions. In contrast, subsequent observation of Phillip showed him to be actively involved in dialogic conversations with the teacher throughout the period of investigation. Thus the consequences of a pupil's positioning within classroom dialogue may be far-reaching in terms of shaping their future participation in the discourse and their sense of agency as learners of mathematics. In the next section we explore the long-term impact of experiencing these different kinds of communicative relationships on students' learner identities and their developing mathematical understanding.

Consolidating identity in secondary school – different groups, different relationships, different understandings

The data in this section are drawn from interviews with girls and boys in years 9 and 10, attending a mixed 11–16 comprehensive in the north west of England. The school places pupils in ability groups for mathematics from the beginning of Year 8, with teaching in mixed ability classes in Year 7, their first year at the school. These data reveal how the differential experiences observed above reappear when we look at secondary school students' accounts of learning mathematics.

Different relationships

The contrast between dialogic and didactic relationships with the teacher that we observed in the primary school sample is also visible in the secondary school sample. It is articulated by the pupils themselves when asked about the role of the teacher in their classes: their replies can be categorised in terms of 'teacher as resource' versus 'teacher as authority', and their occurrence correlates with ability groupings. For example, Michael, who is in Year 9 and is expected to take his GCSE early in Year 10, explains how, in investigative work, he only uses the teacher as a check in discussions which he initiates himself:

> Once we get rolling we're usually quite independent and we'll, once we've checked our answers and then she'll write or we'll run it through her just to make sure she thinks we've gone about the right way of doing it. But that's about it really ... I only ask her as a last resort. I usually ask the people around me first.

Similarly Georgia in Year 9 says that she sometimes tries to work out her own methods, and can find that these are easier than her teacher's suggestions. But she clearly sees the teacher-pupil relationship as one which works best with negotiation on both sides:

> I think you've got to like get on with your teacher, try and see things from their point of view like when you're trying to work something out which makes it easier ... if you have like an idea of what you're going to be doing that's easier because you know like what, you're sort of prepared for it ...[You have to see] like how they're trying to work it out and show you how to work it out.

Georgia and Michael are top set pupils, and their account of the teacher-pupil relationship resonates with that of the other top set students.

Bartholomew's (1999) research also found that teachers of higher ability groups were more likely to focus on pupil learning and involvement with the subject, and to treat pupils as equals, particularly with respect to a subset of (middle-class) boys considered to be 'budding mathematicians' who 'belong there naturally' (Bartholomew, 1999: 14). Lower set pupils, however, report a different relationship altogether. For example, Year 9 Trevor's experience of doing mathematics at school seems to be largely coloured by his perception of the teacher–pupil relationship as being one based on a positional teacher authority. Asked if he ever shares his own ways of solving problems with his teacher, he responds in terms which suggest that the main aim is to avoid a reprimand:

> If we've got the right idea but don't get the right answer, they don't tell us off, still like, at least we've tried.

Whereas top set pupils tend to describe learning as a process of negotiation between teacher and learner, mathematics for Trevor is more like the guessing game identified by many classroom researchers (for example, Edwards and Mercer, 1987; Edwards and Westgate, 1994) in which getting the right answer by any means is the main aim. This contrast is explicitly drawn by Year 10 student Kate, also in the top set, who had been put up 'from the bottom' following a good performance in the Standard Assessment Tasks (SATs) at the end of Year 9. As a result of her experience, Kate strongly believes in effort, but she puts her previous poor behaviour and lack of application down to the teaching she received in lower sets:

> The teacher [is] not very strict, she just sits there, tells us what to do and then just leaves us to do it. She doesn't help us or anything ... That's one of the reasons that I got moved up because Mr Philips saw that I could do it so he took me into his class and he goes through it all ... She'd just sit there even though you'd asked her ... And Mr Philips he'll go through it, he'll come over to you, put attention into you and actually talk you through all the bits you don't understand.

Different understandings

The different experiences of teaching and learning that secondary school pupils report map onto correspondingly different understandings of what mathematics is. As Douglas Barnes has shown in his research, the construction of knowledge is dependent on the ability to make connections, to explore, to think aloud, to be able to make errors and to be able to develop an agentive learner identity. Investigations present an opportunity for a greater sense of ownership and engagement in mathematics, and a corresponding shift in identity, but only the higher ability sub-groups within the classes reported doing these with confidence or enjoyment. Furthermore, students who had been given the opportunity to explore mathematics not just in terms of the tasks they were set but also in terms of how they *talked* about them displayed an understanding of the connections between ideas and concepts within mathematics, in contrast to the more instrumental and rule-driven understandings of those who had experienced less dialogic and more didactic lessons.

An example of how the learning environment can foster an approach to mathematics which looks for and builds on the links between its underlying principles is provided by Georgia, who sees the investigation activity as an opportunity for making such connections, again with the teacher as a resource.

> It won't be the same as anybody else's idea. You get to add like a part of you like into the project or whatever you're doing ... you're using like what you already know and then like adding some bits that maybe you didn't know like with the teacher's help or whatever ... Like if you don't understand something you can try and connect it to something else that you do understand which might make it easier for you to get better at it.

The contrast between different groups and relationships and their impact on identity is summed up by Daniel, who is also in the Year 9 top set. He sees his ability to make connections as something that distinguishes him from other (lower set) pupils.

> I think it's more that I understand maths a bit more than what they do ... like the full picture of maths. They see a little bit like ... seeing as though we're higher we do more of, little bits of more things whereas the people who are lower down do more things with little bits so they don't see as much ... we sort of see it, we sort of see *all* the maths problems and how they connect to each other and we understand it more ... but the other people, they don't understand the more complex things and how they fit into each other.

In contrast, lower set Trevor's basic concern is with his marks. He talks about his performance often, and provides a lot of figures when he is asked about how he did in the recent SATs.

> I'd say I'd got about ... over fifty per cent, like the average, around fifty-eight-ish, something like that. Because the last one I got overall I think was seventy-eight per cent, something sixty-ish ... so I was

pleased with that because my mum said she was happy. At least I got over fifty per cent. And like I'm not bothered that I'd get a low mark as long as I've done better than I think I've done.

Trevor describes mathematics in terms of performance and memory, and he has an instrumental view of its use: he wants to be a truck driver and is focussed on learning the school mathematics necessary for that job and life in general.

I want to be a truck driver so I've got to like see how many hours I've done ... work out the exact mileage and everything ...When I go with my dad and my mum shopping, like buying stuff and it's seventeen point five per cent, they might need to work it out before they go up and buy it ...

These contrasts in the experience of teaching and learning and their corresponding differences in understanding illustrate the development of agentic versus passive or excluded identities. It is no accident of course that these developments take place within the context of ability grouping, itself the embodiment of the emphasis on performance which permeates school structures whether or not teachers want it. As Bartholomew (2000: 6) argues, 'the culture of top set maths groups, and of mathematics more generally, makes it very much easier for some students to believe themselves to be good at the subject than for others'.

The impact of a performance agenda

In this chapter, we have expanded Douglas Barnes's recognition that learners do not necessarily participate in classroom discussions on an equal basis. The data presented demonstrate how the nature of pupil participation correlates with teachers' preconceptions of pupil ability. Furthermore, we have indicated the outcome of such processes by demonstrating that access to 'exploratory talk' really does make a difference to the development of active mathematics learners in comparison to the kind of learner identity that we might otherwise see in many 'traditional' transmission classrooms (Cazden, 2001). In both primary and secondary classrooms, pupils are positioned into, and take up, identities of agency or passivity, and this distinction appears to become more polarised as they progress through the school system and encounter more rigid forms of ability grouping.

As we have argued, mathematics is particularly vulnerable to transmission teaching, and the current emphasis on improving 'performance' means that teachers may be forced to rely on assessing and evaluating pupil input more than ever. Indeed, recent research has highlighted how the literacy and numeracy hours of the English National Curriculum have, in fact, pressurised teachers into using more directive forms of teaching than before, with less emphasis on active learning and consequently fewer opportunities for lower attaining pupils to explore ideas and negotiate misunderstandings (Mroz et al., 2000; English et al., 2002; Smith et al., 2004). In this climate, the strong emphasis on 'performance' is likely to further perpetuate unequal access to the kinds of exploratory talk which have been identified as being valuable to children's learning.

However, such an outcome is not inevitable. As we noted at the beginning of this chapter, Barnes was keen to point out that all learners have the potential to access and benefit from exploratory talk given the right circumstances. A number of interventions in the USA, the UK and Europe have shown that it is possible to promote effective classroom dialogue which develops pupil agency within the constraints outlined above. Jaworski's (2004, 2007) work in Norway provides an example of how teachers and researchers can work together to create possibilities for enabling pupils to inquire into and hence learn mathematics through workshops which introduce mathematical tasks and provide opportunities for all the participants to work together and reflect on their activity and participation. Similarly, Wells's (1999) work on *dialogic inquiry* encouraged teachers to develop small-group work tasks which enable all parties to contribute to the emergent outcomes of an activity (namely, the outcomes are not pre-determined by the teacher) and to collaboratively reach a consensus on what is to be done and why. This, Wells argues, creates a context which 'encourages students critically to examine and evaluate the answers that they make to the questions that interest them and which simultaneously provides an opportunity for their apprenticeship into these "genres of power"' (1999: 264). Success with a similar approach has been demonstrated by Mercer and colleagues on the 'Thinking Together' project in the UK: training children to use exploratory talk in small groups led to improvements not only in the quality of student's reasoning abilities (on Ravens Progressive Matrices) but also in their performance in SATs in Science at age 11 (Mercer et al., 1999; Mercer et al., 2004; Mercer and Dawes (Chapter 4, this volume)). All these approaches have a common emphasis on the role of collaborative relationships in learning – the intention is that knowledge should not be transmitted from teacher to learner in a unidirectional manner, but instead should be collaboratively constructed by all parties.

As we have argued, all learners can benefit from these approaches, and Jo Boaler's recent work (2008) is important in highlighting how interventions aimed at promoting exploratory talk in a climate of collaborative learning are instrumental in developing pupil identities as active mathematics learners in socially deprived areas where expectations regarding student 'performance' are not high. Boaler's research with the students at Railside School (pseudonym) in the USA showed how pedagogic practices which promote 'relational equity' through 'commitment to the learning of others, respectful intellectual relations, and learned methods of communication and support' shape learner identities which are both active and sensitive to the needs of others (Boaler, 2007). These students were also much more likely to continue studying mathematics beyond the boundaries of compulsory schooling. The institutional context is important, however: we recognise that finding the space to implement such 'non-traditional' pedagogic practices is a highly complex matter for teachers and depends very much on the institution and environment in which they are teaching. Nevertheless, the range of projects discussed here demonstrates that there are openings for teachers to negotiate how to improve pupil access to exploratory talk in relation to their own contexts. As Lee (2006: 112) points out in her discussion of changing practice through action research which promotes 'theorised practice':

> Success will not be instant: it will take time for both teacher and pupils to grow accustomed to their changed roles in the classroom – the teacher to managing the learning rather than directing or dictating, the pupils to thinking and articulating their thinking, and taking responsibility for their own learning. In a talking and learning classroom, a discourse community, pupils will come to know that they can use and control mathematical ideas, that they can be mathematicians.

References

Barnes, D. (1976) *From Communication to Curriculum*. Harmondsworth: Penguin.

Barnes, D. and Sheeran, Y. (1992) 'Oracy and genre: speech styles in the classroom', in K. Norman (ed.), *Thinking Voices*. London: Hodder & Stoughton.

Bartholomew, H. (1999) 'Setting in stone? How ability grouping practices structure and constrain achievement in mathematics'. Paper presented at the Annual Conference of the British Educational Research Association. University of Sussex, Brighton.

Bartholomew, H. (2000) 'Negotiating Identity in the Community of the Mathematics Classroom.' Paper presented at the Annual Conference of the British Educational Research Association University of Cardiff. Cardiff: BERA.

Bauersfeld, H. (1995) 'The structuring of structures: development and function of mathematizing as a social practice', in L. Steffe and J. Gale (eds), *Constructivism in Education*. Hillsdale, NJ: Lawrence Erlbaum.

Black, L. (2004a) 'Teacher–pupil talk in whole class discussions and processes of social positioning within the primary school classroom', *Language and Education*, 18 (5): 347–60.

Black, L. (2004b) 'Differential participation in whole class discussions and the construction of marginalised identities', *Journal of Educational Enquiry*, 5 (1): 34–54.

Black, L. (2007) 'Analysing cultural models in socio-cultural discourse analysis', in J. Williams, P.S. Davis and L. Black (eds), *International Journal of Educational Research Special Issue on Subjectivities in School: Socio-cultural and Activity Theory Perspectives*, 46 (1–2): 20–30.

Boaler, J. (1997) 'When even the winners are losers: evaluating the experiences of "top set" students', *Journal of Curriculum Studies*, 29 (2): 65–182.

Boaler, J. (2007) 'Exploring the notion of relational identity'. paper presented at the Fourth ESRC Seminar: Mathematical Relationships: Identities and Participation, University of Wales Institute, Cardiff.

Boaler, J. (2008) 'Promoting relational equity: the mixed ability mathematics approach that taught students high levels of responsibility, respect, and thought', *British Educational Research Journal*, 34(2): 167–94.

Boaler, J., Wiliam, D. and Brown, M. (2000) 'Students' experiences of ability-grouping disaffection, polarisation and the construction of failure', *British Educational Research Journal*, 26 (5): 631–48.

Cazden, C. (2001) *Classroom Discourse: The Language of Teaching and Learning*. Portsmouth, NH: Heinemann.

Cobb, P., Yackel, E. and Wood, T. (1993) 'Discourse, mathematical thinking, and classroom practice', in E. Forman, N. Minick and C. Stone (eds), *Contexts for Learning: Sociocultural Dynamics in Children's Development*. Oxford: Oxford University Press.

de Corte, E., Op't Eynde, P. and Verschaffel, L. (2002) '"Knowing what to believe": the relevance of students' mathematical beliefs for mathematics education', in B. Hofer and P. Pintrich (eds), *Personal Epistemology: The Psychology of Beliefs about Knowledge and Knowing*. Mahwah, NJ: Lawrence Erlbaum.

DfES (2005) 'Success for All', *Standards Unit Newsletter*, Autumn, No. 10. London: DfES.

Edwards, A. and Westgate, D. (1994) *Investigating Classroom Talk*. Abingdon: Falmer.

Edwards, D. and Mercer, N. (1987) *Common Knowledge*. Abingdon: Routledge.

English, E., Hargreaves, L. and Hislam, J. (2002) 'Pedagogical dilemmas in the National Literacy Strategy: primary teachers' perceptions, reflections and classroom behaviour', *Cambridge Journal of Education*, 32 (1): 9–26.

Ireson, J. and Hallam, S. (2001) *Ability Grouping in Education*. London: Paul Chapman Publishing.

Jaworski, B. (2004) 'Learning communities in mathematics: developing and studying inquiry communities in mathematics learning, mathematics teaching and mathematics teaching development'. Paper presented at the British Society for Research into Learning Mathematics. University of Leeds, Leeds.

Jaworski, B. (2007) 'Learning communities in mathematics: research and development in mathematics teaching and learning', in C. Bergsten, B. Grevholm, H.S. Måsoral and F. Rønning (eds.) *Relating Practice and Research in the mathematics education*: Proceedings of NORMA 05, Fourth Nordic Conference on Mathematics Education. Trondheim: Tapir Press.

Lee, C. (2006) *Language for Learning Mathematics*. Maidenhead: Open University Press/McGraw-Hill.

Maher, C.A. (2005) 'How students structure their investigations and learn mathematics: insights from a long-term study', *Journal of Mathematical Behavior* (24): 1–14.

Martino, A.M. and Maher, C.A. (1999) 'Teacher questioning to promote justification and generalization in mathematics: what research has taught us', *Journal of Mathematical Behavior*, (18): 53–78.

Mercer, N. (2000) *Words and Minds: How We Use Language to Think*. Abingdon: Routledge.

Mercer, N., and Fisher, E. (1998) 'How to teachers help children to learn?', in D. Faulkner, K. Littleton and M. Woodhead (eds), *Learning Relationships in the Classroom*. Abingdon: Routledge.

Mercer, N. Wegerif, R. and Dawes, L. (1999) 'Children's talk and the development of reasoning in the classroom', *British Educational Research Journal*, 25 (1): 95–111.

Michaels, S., O'Connor, M., Hall, M. and Resnick, L. (2002) *Accountable Talk: Classroom Conversation that Works* (E-book from CD-ROM Series). Pittsburgh, PA: University of Pittsburgh.

Mroz, M., Smith, F. and Hardman, F. (2000) 'The discourse of the Literacy Hour', *Cambridge Journal of Education*, 30 (3): 379–90.

Myhill, D.A. (2002) 'Bad boys and good girls? Patterns of interaction and response in whole-class teaching', *British Educational Research Journal*, 28 (3): 339–52.

Nathan, M.J. and Knuth, E.J. (2003) 'A study of whole classroom mathematical discourse and teacher change', *Cognition and Instruction*, 21 (2): 175–207.

NCTM (2000) *Principles and Standards for School Mathematics*. Reston, VA: National Council of Teachers of Mathematics.

OFSTED (2006) *Evaluating Mathematics Provision for 14–19-year-olds*. London: Office for Standards in Education.

Reay, D. and Wiliam, D. (1999) '"I'll be a nothing": structure, agency and the construction of identity through assessment', *British Educational Research Journal*, 25 (3): 343–54.

Schoenfeld, A. (1992) 'Learning to think mathematically: problem-solving, metacognition and sense making in mathematics', in D.A. Grouws (ed.), *Handbook of Research on Mathematics Teaching and Learning*. New York: Macmillan.

Smith, F., Hardman, F., Wall, K. and Mroz, M. (2004) 'Interactive whole class teaching in the National Literacy and Numeracy Strategies', *British Educational Research Journal*, 30 (3): 395–411.

Solomon, Y. (2007) 'Experiencing mathematics classes: gender, ability and the selective development of participative identities', in J.S. Williams, P.S. Davis and L. Black (eds), *International Journal of Educational Research Special Issue on Subjectivities in School: Socio-cultural and Activity Theory Perspectives*, 46 (1–2): 8–19.

Solomon, Y. (2008) *Mathematical Literacy: Developing Identities of Inclusion*. New York and London: Routledge.

Wells, G. (1999) *Dialogic Inquiry:Towards a Socio-cultural Practice and Theory of Education*. Cambridge: Cambridge University Press.

Williams, S. and Baxter, J. (1996) 'Dilemmas of discourse-oriented teaching in one middle school mathematics classroom', *The Elementary School Journal*, 97: 21–38.

Culture, Dialogue and Learning: Notes on an Emerging Pedagogy

Robin Alexander

Summary

In this chapter, Robin Alexander draws on his international research on talk in primary classrooms to explain the nature and value of a pedagogic approach called 'dialogic teaching'. The chapter begins with a consideration of the various ways that classroom talk is conceptualised and used by teachers in different countries, and the implications these have for children's participation and learning. He then considers different ways that classroom interaction can be organised and the repertoires teachers can employ when interacting with their pupils. After setting out some principles for dialogic teaching, Alexander then goes on to present some encouraging findings from schools in the UK which have been implementing this approach, and discusses the practical problems and challenges of encouraging its wider implementation.

For Discussion

1   How might understanding the ways in which the role of classroom talk is conceptualised in different countries help us improve the quality of classroom interaction?

(Continued)

(Continued)

2   How might the notion of 'repertoire' (in Alexander's discussion of teachers' interaction with pupils) inform the initial training of teachers?

3   What are the principles underpinning 'dialogic teaching', and what are some of the indicators that it is taking place?

4   What challenges face a teacher who wishes to teach more 'dialogically'?

This chapter[1] is about work in progress on an 'emerging pedagogy' of the spoken word. It is a pedagogy which exploits the power of talk to shape children's thinking and to secure their engagement, learning and understanding. It draws mainly on three areas of my research over the past two decades: first, a large-scale comparative study of the relationship between culture and pedagogy in five countries – England, France, India, Russia and the United States; second, subsequent development work on the idea of 'dialogic teaching'; third, observational research in UK classrooms, which preceded both of these and which ignited my desire to discover whether the identified features and problems of British pedagogy were universal or whether alternatives were available.

The line of enquiry began with observational research during the 1980s and early 1990s (Alexander, 1995: 103–269; Alexander et al., 1996; Alexander, 1997), undertaken at Leeds University (where I was fortunate to be one of Douglas Barnes's colleagues). These projects yielded somewhat dispiriting findings about the character of the talk through which children's learning was being mediated in English primary classrooms. Planning for the international study started in 1992, with the fieldwork undertaken between 1994 and 1998,[2] and the project has a follow-up phase during which I am returning to each of the five countries to explore issues of change and continuity. The main study culminated in a comparative analysis of classroom discourse from the five countries, and pointed the way towards the possibilities of interaction with a dynamic and content which at that time were rarely seen or heard in British classrooms (Alexander, 2001). This work is currently represented in development projects in which I am applying and refining the idea of 'dialogic teaching' with teachers and local authorities in various parts of the UK (Alexander, 2006).

In this chapter I will:

- outline the perspective on classroom talk towards which my international data has steered me;

- outline my idea of dialogic teaching as it currently stands and as teachers in various parts of the UK are at this moment trying to apply it;

- present some interim findings from the schools involved in the dialogic teaching development projects, both positive and problematic.

Contextualising classroom talk

So, to the five-nation 'culture and pedagogy' comparative programme. The work on talk formed part of a three-level macro–micro study – nation, school, classroom – which located the analysis of pedagogy in a prior investigation of educational systems, policies and histories, and of schools as organisations and micro-cultures. At the classroom level, interaction was but one element of teaching which we studied using an ostensibly culture-neutral model, encompassing what we defined as its invariants:

- space;

- student organisation;

- time and pace;

- subject-matter;

- routines, rules and rituals;

- learning task;

- teaching activity;

- student differentiation for teaching;

- teacher assessment of learning.

This contextualising of talk is crucial, as is the wider linking of both discourse and pedagogy to schooling, policy and culture. It must right away be added here that it is the mark of the truly pioneering nature of Douglas Barnes's work, that nearly forty years ago, he was doing pretty well just this. In his 1969 analysis of talk in secondary classrooms, Barnes offered a categorisation of, for example, teachers' questions ('factual', 'reasoning', 'open', 'social', with each subdivided), but he also went much further and explored the dynamics of student participation, social relationships within the classroom, the relationship between language and task, and – especially – the untidy and often uncomprehending meeting of everyday and academic registers. His analysis, then, was above all about the extent to which meaning in classrooms is or more commonly is not conveyed, and about the social meanings with which the academic meanings are entwined. Further, Barnes explicitly discusses, following his colleague Harold Rosen, the 'socio-cultural' and 'conceptual' functions of what is said, and his references include (alongside Flanders) Basil Bernstein (Barnes, 1969: 11–77). Later, but as ever somewhat ahead of the game, he added Vygotsky and Bakhtin (Barnes and Todd, 1995).

The language and cultural constructs of education

Comparative enquiry reminds us that the language of education contains few universals, and educational conversation across cultures is riddled with pitfalls for the unwary. For example, the English word *education* draws out – *educare* – what is already there, but its Russian equivalent, *obrazovanie*, forms something new, and in French, *l'éducation* is closer to the Russian *vospitanie* than it is to the English *education,* which in turn doesn't carry the same overtones of moral and cultural upbringing as either *vospitanie* or *l'éducation*. The English *instruction* is not the same as *obuchenie*, nor is *la formation* as narrowly instrumental as *training,* even though the dictionaries tell us that these French and Russian terms equate: the root of *obuchenie* expands to both *teach* and *learn,* while *formation* hints at the shaping of the person alongside vocational training. In English, *didactic* expresses disapproval, usually of teaching which is expository and by extension is assumed to be authoritarian; elsewhere, *la didactique* and *die Didaktik* celebrate the place in teaching of the subject and its conceptual imperatives. *Development* in English is something that happens naturally, passively, to the child; in Russian it may also imply external agency, a process of intervention by others, with the verb used transitively. And so on. Perhaps, if we want to be Vygotskian about this, we might tentatively suggest that in English – or perhaps in the Anglo-Saxon tradition more generally – such key terms in the educational lexicon veer towards the 'natural line' of development and are more fatalistic and determinist, whereas in the mainstream European tradition they are more suggestive of the 'cultural line', of human perfectibility, and of external agency in human learning.

These terminological shadings are not academic. Subtly, yet profoundly, they may influence how teachers perceive children as learners and their own task as educators. For all, including 'childhood' itself, are cultural constructs, and the power differential of classrooms makes it virtually impossible for children to resist these constructs' typificatory consequences (Alexander, 1984), especially when classroom interaction is too limited or one-sided to provide the teacher with contrary evidence about what kind of a person each of their students really is.

The place of talk in the curriculum and in teaching

With these shifting terminological sands in mind, consider for example the educational place of talk itself in the curriculum and, generically, in teaching across the curriculum. On this side of the Dover Straits we have England's traditional and unchanging definition of the educational 'basics' as reading, writing and calculation, but emphatically not speaking. On the other side, French schools celebrate the primacy of the spoken word. Here, literacy: there, language. And while literacy is defined in England as a 'basic skill', in France it reflects a confident and more elevated nexus of linguistic skills, literary knowledge, republican values and civic virtues. The citizen is one who speaks, reasons and argues on the basis of a broad education, not merely someone who reads and writes with tolerable competence and swallows the myth that Britain is a democracy.

Further, England has nothing like the tradition of oral pedagogy which is fundamental to public education in many continental European countries. In England the default learning task is writing, writing and more writing (yet, as employers and universities frequently complain, all this endless practice does not make anything approaching perfect). It is true that things are changing, not least in response to the efforts of Douglas Barnes and others whose work appears in this book, but change has been slow, and established habits of thought can be hard to shift.

Versions of human relations

The place of talk in teaching is about more than this though, and again we must be alert to values. If 'speaking and listening skills' are unacceptably reductionist, then we must also avoid the technicist overtones of 'oral pedagogy', for talk is relational as well as communicative (as, once again, Barnes noted in the 1960s). Our international evidence shows how within both the wider context of education and the more specific domain of teaching, ideas about how people should relate to each other are paramount. Teachers in the five-nation study articulated, enacted, or steered an uncertain path between three versions of human relations: *individualism*, *community* and *collectivism*.

- *Individualism* puts the self above others and personal rights before collective responsibilities. It emphasises the unconstrained freedom of thought and action.

- *Community* centres on human interdependence, caring for others, sharing and collaborating.

- *Collectivism* also emphasises human interdependence, but only in so far as it serves the larger needs of society, or the state (the two are not identical), as a whole.

Within the observed classrooms, a commitment to *individualism* was manifested in intellectual or social differentiation, divergent rather than uniform learning outcomes, and a view of knowledge as being personal and unique rather than imposed from above in the form of disciplines or subjects. *Community* was reflected in collaborative learning tasks, often in small groups, in 'caring and sharing' rather than competing, and in an emphasis on the affective rather than the cognitive. *Collectivism* was reflected in common knowledge, common ideals, a single curriculum for all, national culture rather than pluralism and multi-culture, and on learning together rather than in isolation or in small groups.

These values were pervasive at national, school and classroom levels. We are familiar with the contrast between the supposedly egocentric cultures of the west, with the USA as the gas-guzzling arch villain, and the supposedly holistic, sociocentric cultures of south and east Asia. Though there is evidence to support this opposition (Shweder, 1991), it is all too easy to demonise one pole and romanticise – or orientalise – the other. But I think when it comes to pedagogy the tripartite distinction holds up, and it seems by no means accidental that so much discussion of teaching methods should have centred on the relative merits of whole-class teaching, group and individual work.

In France, this debate can be traced back to arguments at the start of the nineteenth century about the relative merits of *l'enseignement simultané*, *l'enseignement mutuel* and *l'enseignement individuel* (Reboul-Scherrer, 1989).[3] As a post-revolutionary instrument for fostering civic commitment and national identity as well as literacy, *l'enseignement simultané* won. Only now, reflecting decentralisation and the rising tide of individualism, has its hegemony in France begun to be questioned. In contrast, it seems by no means accidental that after years of rejection by England's teachers as authoritarian and indoctrinatory, something called 'interactive whole-class teaching' should have found favour as the British government's preferred tool for implementing its national numeracy and literacy strategies.

Individualism, community and collectivism – or child, group and class – are the organisational nodes of pedagogy, not just for reasons of practical exigency but because they are the social and indeed political nodes of human relations. Such differences profoundly influence the dynamics and communicative relationships of classroom talk. If a teacher arranges desks in a horseshoe or square so that each child can see and interact with all the others as well as with herself, and sits with the children rather than stands apart from them, she provokes a different kind of talk, and intimates a different pedagogical relationship, to that signalled by having separate desks in rows facing the front, whereby children can establish eye-contact with the teacher but not with each other, and the teacher stands while the children sit.

Versions of teaching

Alongside these three relational values there emerged from our data a second set. Where individualism, community and collectivism start with the relationship of individuals to society and each other, and move from there into the classroom, the six pedagogical values start with the purposes of education, the nature of knowledge and the relationship of teacher and learner.

- *Teaching as transmission* sees education primarily as a process of instructing children to absorb, replicate and apply basic information and skills.

- *Teaching as initiation* sees education as the means of providing access to, and passing on from one generation to the next, the culture's stock of high-status knowledge, for example in literature, the arts, the humanities and the sciences.

- *Teaching as negotiation* reflects the Deweyan idea that teachers and students jointly create knowledge and understanding rather than relate to one another as an authoritative source of knowledge and its passive recipient.

- *Teaching as facilitation* guides the teacher by principles which are developmental (and, more specifically, Piagetian) rather than cultural or epistemological. The teacher respects and nurtures individual differences, and waits until children are ready to move on instead of pressing them to do so.

- *Teaching as acceleration*, in contrast, implements the Vygotskian principle that education is planned and guided acculturation rather than facilitated 'natural' development, and indeed that the teacher seeks to outpace development rather than follow it.

- *Teaching as technique*, finally, is relatively neutral in its stance on society, knowledge and the child. Here the important issue is the efficiency of teaching regardless of the context of values, and to that end imperatives like structure, the economic use of time and space, carefully graduated tasks, regular assessment and clear feedback are more pressing than ideas such as democracy, autonomy, development or the disciplines.

The value systems applied: classroom talk

How does all this relate to classroom talk? Well, the collective ambience of Russian and French classrooms and the dominance of whole-class teaching were buttressed there by the collective and very public nature of teacher–pupil exchanges: children were expected to talk clearly, loudly and expressively, and they learned very early on to do so. Further, because both knowledge transmission and cultural initiation were explicit educational goals, the distinctive registers and vocabularies of different subjects were firmly and consistently applied, and language was no less rule-bond than personal conduct.

In contrast, in many of the American classrooms antipathy towards transmission teaching pushed interaction into an unfailingly questioning mode, whether or not it was appropriate, while objections to the hegemony of school subjects created a situation where children individually expressed their own mathematical meanings, say, but lacked a common language collectively to make sense of and evaluate them. Indeed, in a climate of sometimes extreme relativism any 'version' of knowledge might be accepted whether or not it made sense and all answers might be deemed equally valid. Talk, overall, had a markedly conversational ambience and tone. The teachers themselves defined it thus, usually by reference to negotiated pedagogy and the importance of 'sharing' – the notion of the class as a community – whereas in interview some Russian teachers explicitly distinguished conversation from dialogue and highlighted their role in fostering that dialogue.

So the critical questions here concern not so much the *tone* of the discourse as its meaning and where it leads. I want to stay with that stipulative distinction between 'conversation' and 'dialogue', which is all the more necessary when most dictionaries treat the two as synonymous. Where the end point of conversation may not be clear at the outset, in classroom dialogue, for the teacher at least, it usually is. Where conversation often consists of a sequence of unchained, two-part exchanges as participants talk at or past each other (though it *can* be very different), classroom dialogue explicitly seeks to make attention and engagement mandatory and to chain exchanges into a meaningful sequence.

In fact, much of the interaction that we recorded in English primary classrooms was neither conversation nor dialogue. Thus:

- Interactions tended to be brief rather than sustained, and teachers moved from one child to another in rapid succession in order to maximise participation, or from one question to another in the interests of maintaining pace, rather than developing sustained and incremental lines of thinking and understanding.

- Teachers asked questions about content, but children's questions were confined to points of procedure.

- Closed questions predominated.

- Children concentrated on identifying 'correct' answers, and teachers glossed over 'wrong' answers rather than using them as stepping stones to understanding.

- There was little speculative talk, or 'thinking aloud'.

- That the questions were – in Nystrand's terms – 'test' rather than 'authentic' (Nystrand et al., 1997) was further demonstrated by the fact that teachers gave children time to recall but less commonly gave them time to think.

- The child's answer marked the end of an exchange, and the teacher's feedback closed it.

- Feedback tended to encourage and praise rather than to inform, and in such cases the cognitive potential of exchanges was lost.

Versions of communicative competence

Though in the real world communicative competence may be defined by reference to the Gricean maxims of *quantity, quality, relation* and *manner* (Grice, 1975), in classrooms the unequal power relationship of teacher and taught may produce a very different set of rules. For students, they are dominated by listening, bidding for turns, spotting 'correct' answers, and other coping strategies which anywhere outside of school would seem pretty bizarre.

Since this tendency was identified by Philip Jackson and others forty years ago (Holt, 1964; Jackson, 1968), one might suppose that this is the way, everywhere, that classrooms inevitably are. It isn't. Our international data show that these so-called 'rules' of communicative competence, which have come mainly out of British and American classroom research (Edwards and Westgate, 1994), are neither universal nor inevitable and that they can be subverted by genuine discussion or by a version of whole-class teaching which is rather different from the classic British and American recitation teaching of 'test' questions, minimal 'uptake' and evaluative but otherwise uninformative feedback.

Again, France and Russia provide useful counterpoints. The English tradition emphasises the importance of the equal distribution of teacher time and attention among all the pupils, and participation by all of them in oral work, in every lesson. So with only one teacher and 20–30 pupils in a class it is inevitable that competitive bidding and the gamesmanship of 'guess what teacher is thinking', and above all searching for the 'right' answer, become critical to a pupil's getting by. But in many of the Russian lessons we observed, only a proportion of children were expected to contribute orally in a given lesson. Here, instead of eliciting a succession of brief 'now or never' answers from many children, the teacher constructs a sequence of much more sustained exchanges with a smaller number. Because the ambience is collective rather than individualised or collaborative, each child talks to the class as much as to the teacher and is in a sense a representative of that class as much as an individual. This reduces the element of communicative gamesmanship, but it also – crucially – may prove a more powerful learning tool. And because there is time to do more than parrot the expected answer, the talk is more likely to probe children's thinking, and indeed in such settings it is common to see children coming to the blackboard and explaining the way they have worked through a problem while the other children listen, look and learn (though of course not always).

Such differences provoke an important question. From what pattern of classroom exchange do children learn more: questioning involving many children, brief answers and little follow-up, or questions directed at fewer children that invite longer and more considered answers which in turn lead to further questions? In one scenario, children bid for turns if they know the answer, or try to avoid being nominated if they do not; in the other, they listen to each other. In the English approach, communicative competence is defined by whether, having been nominated for or having bid for what is probably one's sole oral contribution to the lesson, one provides an answer which the teacher judges to be acceptable or relevant. In the alternative approach, communicative competence is judged by how one performs over the whole transaction rather than whether one gives the single 'right' answer; and also by the *manner* of the response – clarity, articulateness, attention to the question – as well as its substance.

Towards dialogic teaching: repertoires, principles and indicators

I said at the beginning of this chapter that the collective, extended and cumulative kinds of interaction which I recorded outside the UK during the late 1990s were at that time rarely encountered in England, but that things are changing. They are changing partly because of the UK government's national strategies' somewhat muddled emulation – in the form of 'interactive whole-class teaching' – of what I and others have recorded, and partly because in England, as in the USA, there is a growing band of people for whom the notion of 'dialogue' crystallises what the evidence on learning shows is most urgently needed, and what the evidence on teaching shows is most palpably absent. In other words, a movement is gathering momentum.

Here then is the essence, though not the detail, of the approach on which I have been working since completing the *Five Cultures* research (see Alexander, 2006, for a fuller account). In this, the idea of *repertoire* is paramount. The varied objectives of teaching cannot be achieved through a single approach or technique (and in case it seems that I have a rosy view of Russian pedagogy, I would also add here that it can be as unproductively monolithic as teaching anywhere else, and indeed often is. My main reason for citing Russia is because it offers such a striking contrast to approaches with which we are more familiar). Instead, teachers need a repertoire of approaches from which they can select on the basis of fitness for purpose in relation to the learner, the subject-matter and the opportunities and constraints of the context. The idea of repertoire can be extended infinitely, down to the finest nuance of discourse. But to make it manageable, we must concentrate in the first instance on three broad aspects of pedagogical interaction: *organisation*, *teaching talk* and *learning talk*.

Repertoire 1: organising interaction

The *organisational* repertoire comprises five broad interactive possibilities reflecting our earlier distinction between individualism, community and collectivism, or child, group and class.

- *Whole-class teaching* in which the teacher relates to the class as a whole, and individual students relate to the teacher and to each other collectively.

- *Collective group work* in which group work is led by the teacher and is therefore a scaled-down version of whole-class teaching.

- *Collaborative group work* in which the teacher sets a task on which children must work together, and then withdraws.

- *One-to-one activity* in which the teacher works with individual children.

- *One-to-one activity* in which children work in pairs.

Thus the organisational possibilities are whole class, group and individual, but group and individual interaction subdivide according to whether it is steered by the teacher or the children themselves. A competent teacher, I would argue, needs to able to manage all five kinds of interaction, and to select from them as appropriate.

Repertoire 2: teaching talk

The teaching talk repertoire comprises the five kinds of talk we observed in use across the five countries in the international study. First, we have the three most frequently used.

- *Rote* which is the drilling of facts, ideas and routines through constant repetition.

- *Recitation* which is the accumulation of knowledge and understanding through questions designed to test or stimulate the recall of what has been previously encountered, or to cue students to work out the answer from clues provided in the question.

- *Instruction/exposition* which is telling the student what to do, and/or imparting information, and/or explaining facts, principles or procedures.

These provide the familiar and traditional bedrock of teaching by direct instruction. Less frequently, but no less universally, we find some teachers also using the two other kinds.

- *Discussion* which is the exchange of ideas with a view to sharing information and solving problems.

- *Dialogue* which is achieving common understanding through structured, cumulative questioning and discussion which guide and prompt, reduce choices, minimise risk and error, and expedite the 'handover' of concepts and principles.

Each of these, even rote, has its place in the teaching of a modern and variegated curriculum, but the last two – discussion and dialogue – are less frequently found than the first three. Yet discussion and dialogue are the forms of talk which are most in line with prevailing thinking on children's learning.

It is important to note that there is no necessary connection between the first and second repertoires. That is to say, whole-class teaching does not have to be dominated by rote and recitation, and discussion is not confined to group work.

Repertoire 3: learning talk

This third repertoire is the child's rather than the teacher's. It constitutes not how the teacher talks or organises interaction, but how the children themselves talk, and the forms of oral expression and interaction which they need to experience and eventually master. This *learning talk* repertoire includes the ability to:

- narrate

- explain

- instruct

- ask different kinds of question

- receive, act and build upon answers

- analyse and solve problems

- speculate and imagine

- explore and evaluate ideas

- discuss

- argue, reason and justify

- negotiate.

together with four contingent abilities or dispositions which are vital if children are to gain the full potential of talking with others:

- listen

- be receptive to alternative viewpoints

- think about what they hear

- give others time to think.

Learning talk repertoires such as this – and others are clearly possible, depending on how one conceives of human development on the one hand and the curriculum on the other – are often missing from the discussion of classroom interaction. Because the teacher controls the talk, researchers tend to start and finish there, focussing on teacher questions, statements, instructions and evaluations and how children respond to them, rather than on the kinds of talk which children themselves need to encounter and engage in.

Principles of dialogic teaching

So far we have had a view of classroom talk which requires a judicious selection from three repertoires – organisation, teaching talk and learning talk. Now we come to the heart of the matter. I submit that teaching which is dialogic rather than transmissive, and which provides the best chance for children to develop the diverse learning talk repertoire on which different kinds of thinking and understanding are predicated, meets five criteria. Such teaching is:

- *collective* in that teachers and children address learning tasks together, whether as a group or as a class;

- *reciprocal* in that teachers and children listen to each other, share ideas and consider alternative viewpoints;

- *supportive* in that children articulate their ideas freely, without the fear of embarrassment over 'wrong' answers, and help each other to reach common understandings;

- *cumulative* in that teachers and children build on their own and each other's ideas and chain them into coherent lines of thinking and enquiry;

- *purposeful* in that teachers plan and steer classroom talk with specific educational goals in view.

The genealogy of these principles is complex, and I would need another chapter to elucidate it in full. Suffice it to say that it combines (i) a positive response to what I and others have observed by way of effective classroom interaction in the UK and elsewhere; (ii) an attempt to counter the less satisfactory features of mainstream classroom interaction (which, for example, tends not to exploit the full collective potential of children working in groups and classes, is one-sided rather than reciprocal, is fragmented or circular rather than cumulative, and is often unsupportive of or even intimidating to all but the most confident child); (iii) a distillation of ideas from others working in this and related fields.

Thus, the definition of *dialogue* in the teaching talk repertoire owes much to Bruner's ideas on scaffolding and 'handover' (Bruner, 1978, 1995). The criterion of *reciprocity* relates to Palincsar and Brown (1984) on 'reciprocal teaching' and to more recent work on communities of learning and practice (Lave and Wenger, 1991; Rogoff et al., 2001), while *cumulation* echoes Bakhtin's powerful confirmation of the condition on which both individual learning and the advancement of collective human understanding critically depend: 'If an answer does not give rise to a new question from itself, it falls out of the dialogue' (Bakhtin, 1986: 168).

In fact, if any utterance deserves epigrammatic status in the context of dialogic teaching it is Bakhtin's, though alongside it we might place Nystrand's empirically-based judgement that 'the bottom line for learning' is 'the extent to which [teaching] requires students to think, not just to report someone else's thinking' (Nystrand et al., 1997: 72).

Incidentally, Skidmore claims that this approach is over-cerebral and neglects the affective aspects of children's learning (Skidmore, 2006). I do not accept this: the first three principles, and especially the third, are directed towards establishing a climate which maximises the power of collective endeavour but also attends closely to how children feel when working and talking with others. The classroom evidence reported below, especially as it relates to those children who are less able or who lack confidence, underlines this.

Indicators of dialogic teaching

The final element in our framework for dialogic teaching is a set of classroom indicators which help teachers to get the conditions right for talk which meets the five criteria, and to consider how best to structure and manage the different kinds of teaching and learning talk in the various organisational formats which are available – whole class, group, individual. There are some 61 of these indicators (all detailed in Alexander, 2006) and they enlist the various aspects of teaching in the *Culture and Pedagogy* framework I referred to earlier – space, time, student organisation, lesson structure, assessment and so on – in support of the dialogic pursuit. Our approach encourages teachers to think, plan and act in a more holistic fashion.

Two development projects

In the London and Yorkshire dialogic teaching development projects, different strategies are being used to meet identical ends – the fostering of the extended repertoires of organisation, teaching talk and learning talk which I have outlined, and achieving the shift in the dynamics, structure and content of such talk which is necessary for the dialogic criteria to be met.

At the same time, teachers in both local authorities are using video to study and evaluate their practice, to record the baselines from which it develops, and to identify aspects of the talk in those classrooms on which they need to work. The bonus of using video is that in several classrooms it has become a powerful teaching tool. Observing the camera observing them, many children have asked to see the videotapes and, naturally, have commented on what they see and hear. Some teachers have decided to exploit this interest and have built video analysis by children into their language teaching. We now have evidence of growing meta-linguistic awareness among these children as they discuss with increasing sophistication and sensitivity the dynamics and mechanisms of interaction: the use of eye contact, listening, taking turns, handling the dominant individual and supporting the reticent one, engaging with what others say rather than merely voicing one's own opinions, and so on.

The two projects are being evaluated formatively and – later – summatively, using a combination of observation, interview, video analysis and, as a relatively stable outcome measure in the North Yorkshire project, performance in national Key Stage 2 tests in English and mathematics. These videotapes provide an evaluative baseline for the project as a whole, as well as for each of its participating teachers. Only three years into one of the projects and two years into the other, we cannot read too much into the albeit encouraging trends in test scores, and for the time being must rely more on the process data.

Interim findings

The Yorkshire year-on-year process data (Alexander, 2003, 2004) offers evidence of the following changes:

- There is more talking about talk, by children as well as teachers.

- Teachers and children are devising ground rules for the management of discussion.

- Teachers are making their questions more focussed yet more genuinely open than hitherto, and are reducing their reliance on questions which cue a specific response.

- There is a discernible shift in questioning strategies away from competitive hands-up bidding to the nominating of particular children, and questions are being formulated more with these children's individual capacities in mind.

- Teachers are giving children more thinking time, and are reducing the pressure on them to provide instant responses.

- Children are answering more loudly, clearly and confidently, and at greater length.

- Children are speculating, thinking aloud and helping each other, rather than competing to spot the 'right' answer.

- Teachers are avoiding the over-use of the stock response to children's contributions of merely repeating or reformulating them but doing nothing further with them.

- Teachers and children are beginning to build on questions and answers, by adopting a questioning strategy of extension (staying with one child or theme) rather than rotation (questioning round the class).

- In discussion, children are listening more carefully and respectfully to each other, and are talking collectively to a common end rather than at or past each other.

- There is greater involvement of less able children, who are finding that the changed dynamics of classroom talk provide them with alternative opportunities to show competence and progress, and of those quiet, compliant children 'in the middle' who are often inhibited by unfocused questioning, the competitiveness of bidding and the dominance of some of their peers. The interactive culture in these classrooms is becoming more inclusive.

- The reading and writing of all children, especially the less able, are benefitting from this greater emphasis on talk, thus confirming that the traditional English idea of literacy without oracy makes little sense. Frequently, this gain is most strikingly noted in the context of lessons in which the proportion of time spent on oral and written tasks is changed to allow more discussion and a shorter but more concentrated period of writing. This, incidentally, is more like the continental, episodic lesson trajectory which we observed in the *Culture and Pedagogy* research.

And from the London project (Alexander, 2005):

- Teachers are constructing their questions more carefully. Questions starting with 'What?', 'Who?' and 'How many?' are giving way to those starting with 'Why?' and 'How?'. Teachers, then, are balancing factual recall or test questions with those that probe thinking and encourage analysis and speculation. 'Now who can tell me ... ?' questions, and competitive hands-up bidding to answer them, are being used more discriminatingly.

- Student–teacher exchanges are becoming longer.

- Student answers are less likely to be merely repeated, and more likely to be built upon.

- Teachers are directing and controlling discussion less, and prompting and facilitating it more.

- There is a more flexible mix of recitation, exposition and discussion.

- Information and opinion – rather than yet more questions – are being used to take students' thinking forward, so the balance of questioning and exposition is changing.

- Students are showing a growing confidence in oral pedagogy: more are speaking readily, clearly and audibly.

- Students are offering longer responses to teacher questions.

- Student contributions are becoming more diverse: instead of just factual recall there are now contributions of an expository, explanatory, justificatory or speculative kind.

- There is more pupil–pupil talk.

- More pupils are taking the initiative and commenting or asking their own questions.

Challenges

All of this is encouraging, and some of it is exemplified on the DVD we have made to support the work of the North Yorkshire schools. This uses sequences from complete lessons, naturalistically filmed without rehearsal or repetition, to illustrate the different kinds of talk in the dialogic repertoire listed earlier, in both group and whole-class contexts (North Yorkshire County Council, 2006). But it is far from plain sailing, and we need to be honest about the problems we are encountering in attempting to encourage what, in British class-rooms, is in effect a transformation of the culture of talk and atten-dant assumptions about the relationship of teacher and taught.

First, as with all innovation, there is a gap between those teachers who are achieving real change and those whose practice has shifted rather less. That gap is increasing, for success fuels both understand-ing and conviction.

Second, although children are being given more time to think through their responses to questions, and are more frequently encouraged to provide extended answers, it is rather less common to find the remain-ing conditions being met: that is, that answers should be responded to in a way that helps the child and/or the class to learn from what has been said. It remains the case that after such extended responses the feedback is often minimal and judgemental ('Excellent', 'Good girl', 'Not quite what I was looking for' or the not-so-ambiguous 'Ye-es ... ') rather than informative. Apart from failing to exploit a critical moment in the dialogic exchange, teachers providing this traditional form of feedback are probably also signalling an equally traditional message to their pupils: that in the end, though there is now more time to think, and space to provide a fuller answer, the answers which count are still those that the teacher expects, and extended thinking time is not so much for thinking from first principles as for deducing even more accurately than hitherto what it is that the teacher wishes to hear. In other words, extended talk and dialogic talk are not the same, and the most frequently observed kind of teacher–pupil talk still remains closer to recitation than to dialogue.

Third, teachers are striving to extend their repertoire of teacher talk, but as yet rather less attention is being given to the repertoire of *learning talk*, and the systematic building of children's capacities to narrate, explain, instruct, question, respond, build upon responses, analyse, speculate, explore, evaluate, discuss, argue, reason, justify and negotiate, and to judge when each form of talk is most appropriate. This means that the intellectual and social empowerment which dialogic teaching can offer may remain limited, even when in other respects talk displays dialogic properties.

Fourth, our efforts to shift from monolithic to repertoire-based models of teaching and classroom interaction have confirmed even more strongly than previously that recitation remains the default teaching mode. It takes little for 'test' questions to reassert their historic dominance, for children's contributions to regress to the monosyllabic or dutiful, and for feedback to become once again phatic or uninformative. Nomination, extended thinking time and longer answers are all a step in the right direction, but dialogue requires an interactive loop or spiral rather than linearity. A long answer is not enough. It is what happens to the answer that makes it worth uttering, and transforms it from a correct or incorrect response to a cognitive stepping stone.

Fifth, our evidence shows that one of the criteria – cumulation – is much more difficult to achieve than the others, yet it is perhaps the most important one of all. The first three (collectivity, reciprocity and support) are essentially concerned with the *conduct* and *ethos* of classroom talk. The other two (cumulation and purposefulness) are no less concerned with its *content*. Working with teachers has shown that we can dramatically change the dynamics and ethos of classroom talk by making it more collective, reciprocal and supportive, and by setting out the 'rules for speaking and listening' which translate these principles into guidelines which children will understand and identify with. The dynamics and climate of talk will then begin to change, and often quite quickly.

But what of the content and meaning of talk, as opposed to its dynamics? Cumulation is possibly the toughest of the five principles of dialogic teaching. Collectivity, reciprocity and support require us to rethink classroom organisation and relationships. But cumulation simultaneously makes demands on a teacher's professional skill, subject knowledge, and insight into the capacities and current understanding of each of his/her pupils. Except in a context where teachers take a strictly relativist view of knowledge (such as we encountered in several of the *Culture and Pedagogy* American classrooms), cumulation requires a teacher to match discourse to learner while respecting the form and modes of enquiry and validation of the subject being taught, seeking then to scaffold understanding between the child's and the culture's ways of making sense. This issue is now being explored by Cazden through a comparative study of mathematical discourse in classrooms in Singapore and the USA (Cazden, 2005).

Compounding the challenge, cumulation also tests a teacher's ability to receive and review what has been said and to judge what to offer by way of an individually-tailored response which will take learners' thinking forward – all in the space of a few seconds – hundreds of times each day.

So although the five dialogic teaching principles or criteria are intended to be taken as a package, for none of them is dispensable, it is probably helpful to teacher development to divide them into two groups, and this is what we have started working on. If we want to make the transformation of classroom talk achievable for other than the most talented teachers, we might concentrate first on getting the ethos, dynamics and affective climate right: that is, by making talk collective, reciprocal and supportive. In those classrooms where these conditions and qualities are established, we can then attend more closely to the other two principles. Here, we can identify the purposes of the talk and use cumulation to steer it towards those purposes. We can work on listening to and building on answers and getting children to do the same. We can reflect on the feedback we provide. We can reassess the balance of drawing out (questioning) and putting in (exposition). We can consider how ideas are not merely *exchanged* in an encouraging and supportive climate but also *built upon*.

There is a final challenge, and it underscores our earlier discussion of the need to relate the analysis of classroom talk to its contexts of pedagogy, policy and culture. Notwithstanding the appropriation of dialogic teaching by the Qualifications and Curriculum Authority (QCA) and the national strategies, some of our teachers feel that dialogic teaching's collective classroom ethic, and its emphasis on reciprocity and mutuality in learning, are being increasingly compromised by current government policy. In a culture of high stakes testing, which the UK government insists is here to stay, competition replaces collaboration while coaching for recall against the clock subverts speculation, debate and divergence. Meanwhile, the emphasis on personalisation and choice may make the recent British espousal of the idea of classrooms as learning communities somewhat short-lived.

Perhaps, therefore, the bowdlerisation of dialogic teaching by official agencies reflects not so much a failure to understand what it is about as a conscious attempt to force it to fit a framework, and a view of education, with which it is not really compatible. For it is hard to see how learning as dialogue can sit other than uncomfortably with teaching as compliance.

References

Alexander, R.J. (1984) *Primary Teaching*. London: Cassell.

Alexander, R.J. (1995) *Versions of Primary Education*. Abingdon: Routledge.

Alexander, R.J. (1997) *Policy and Practice in Primary Education: Local Initiative, National Agenda*. Abingdon: Routledge.

Alexander, R.J. (2001) *Culture and Pedagogy: International Comparisons in Primary Education*. Oxford: Blackwell.

Alexander, R.J. (2003) *Talk for Learning: The First Year*. Northallerton: North Yorkshire County Council.

Alexander, R.J. (2004) *Talk for Learning: The Second Year*. Northallerton: North Yorkshire County Council.

Alexander, R.J. (2005) *Teaching Through Dialogue: The First Year*. London: London Borough of Barking and Dagenham.

Alexander, R.J. (2006) *Towards Dialogic Teaching: Rethinking Classroom Talk* (third edition). York: Dialogos.

Alexander, R.J., Willcocks, J. and Nelson, N. (1996) 'Discourse, pedagogy and the National Curriculum: change and continuity in primary schools', *Research Papers in Education*, 11 (1): 81–120.

Bakhtin, M. (1986) *Speech Genres and Other Essays*. Austin, TX: University of Texas Press.

Barnes, D. (1969) 'Language in the secondary classroom', in D. Barnes, J. Britton, and H. Rosen (eds), *Language, the Learner and the School*. Harmondsworth: Penguin.

Barnes, D. and Todd, F. (1995) *Communication and Learning Revisited*. Portsmouth, NH, Heinemann.

Bruner, J.S. (1978) 'The role of dialogue in language acquisition', in A. Sinclair, R. Jarvella and W. Levelt (eds), *The Child's Conception of Language*. New York: Springer-Verlag.

Bruner, J.S. (1995) 'Vygotsky: a historical and conceptual perspective', in J.V. Wertsch (ed.), *Culture, Communication and Cognition: Vygotskian Perspectives*. Cambridge: Cambridge University Press.

Cazden, C.B. (2005) 'The value of eclecticism in education reform'. Paper presented at the AERA Annual Meeting.

Edwards, A.D. and Westgate, D.P.G. (1994) *Investigating Classroom Talk*, (second edition). Abingdon: Falmer.

Grice, H.P. (1975) 'Logic and conversation', in P. Cole and J. Morgan (eds), *Syntax and Semantics*, Volume 3, *Speech Acts*. New York: Academic.

Holt, J. (1964) *How Children Fail*. London: Pitman.

Jackson, P.W. (1968) *Life in Classrooms*. New York: Holt, Rinehart and Winston.

Lave, J. and Wenger, E. (1991) *Situated Learning: Legitimate Peripheral Participation*. Cambridge: Cambridge University Press.

North Yorkshire County Council, with Robin Alexander (consultant and script) (2006) *Talk for Learning: Teaching and Learning Through Dialogue*. Northallerton: North Yorkshire County Council (DVD/CD pack: for ordering details go to www.robinalexander.org. uk/dialogos.htm).

Nystrand, M., Gamoran, A., Kachur, R. and Prendergast, C. (1997) *Opening Dialogue: Understanding the Dynamics of Language and Learning in the English Classroom*. New York: Teachers College Press.

Palincsar, A.S. and Brown, A.L. (1984) *Reciprocal Teaching of Comprehension Fostering and Monitoring Activities: Cognition and Instruction*. Hillsdale, NJ: Lawrence Erlbaum.

Reboul-Scherrer, F. (1989) *Les Premiers Instituteurs, 1833–1882*. Paris: Hachette.

Rogoff, B., Turkanis, C.G. and Bartlett, L. (eds) (2001) *Learning Together: Children and Adults in a School Community*. New York: Oxford University Press.

Shweder, R.A. (1991) *Thinking Through Cultures: Expeditions in Cultural Psychology*. Cambridge: Harvard University Press.

Skidmore, D. (2006) 'Pedagogy and dialogue', *Cambridge Journal of Education*, 36 (4): 503–14.

Notes

1   This is an abridged version of a keynote paper given at the tenth international conference of the International Association for Cognitive Education and Psychology (IACEP) in 2005.

2   *Primary Education in Five Cultures*, funded by the Leverhulme Trust and reported in Alexander, 2001.

3   'Simultaneous', 'mutual' and 'individual' correspond to whole-class teaching, collaborative [group] work and one-to-one teaching, even though at the time *l'enseignement mutuel* was more about the application of the Lancasterian monitorial system.

7

Talking Texts Into Being: on the Social Construction of Everyday Life and Academic Knowledge in the Classroom

Judith Green, Beth Yeager and
Maria Lucia Castanheira

Summary

This chapter reviews the ethnographic approach developed by members of the Santa Barbara Classroom Discourse Group. The authors explain how this approach has helped them to shed light on how classroom 'life' shapes and is shaped by the learning discourses of the teachers, students and the wider community. Drawing upon extracts from essays written by students, they relate acts of learning to the developing language and dialogue of the classroom. They argue that students develop a 'dialogue of learning' which is based upon their own agency (point of view), an emergent intertextuality (dialogue that is socially and academically significant for the student), and by the construction of rich points (junctions in dialogic interaction that mark unexpected events or propositions). The authors conclude that social constructs found in student texts are a valuable way of mapping emergent ways of their thinking and negotiation of meaning.

> ### For Discussion
>
> 1 What do the authors mean by the language of the classroom?
> 2 The authors refer to the concept of 'common knowledge' first developed by Edwards and Mercer, but what is the common knowledge in this context?
> 3 To what extent does having a different home and school discourse impact on how students learn in the classroom?
> 4 The authors introduce the concept of 'rich points' as unexpected moments that occur in the discourse of the classroom, but how does this relate to the concept of dialogic interaction?

This chapter is entitled *Talking Texts into Being*; however, it might equally have been entitled, *Learning to See Learning Processes in Classrooms*, given Douglas Barnes's argument that to study the language of the classroom is to study both the learning processes and some of the internal and external constraints upon it (Barnes, 1969). In arguing that the study of language is ultimately the study of learning processes, Douglas Barnes proposed a new way of thinking about the relationship of language and learning processes in classrooms. This conceptual argument has brought challenges to teachers, researchers, students and visitors to classrooms for the past four decades, and is today as challenging as it was when he first framed it – how to see what's happening in the classroom as members do (Barnes, 1969: 12).

In this chapter, we describe the ethnographic perspective that members of our research community, the Santa Barbara Classroom Discourse Group, have developed over the past three decades to explore this very question – What's happening here? This research community was created in 1990 and continues today. In this community, teachers, students and university-based ethnographers work collaboratively to examine what is happening in the classroom and how the language and practices of the classroom are consequential for student learning of academic processes. (e.g., Santa Barbara Classroom Discourse Group, 1992a; b; Green and Dixon, 1993; Yeager et al., 1998; Castanheira, 2004; Dixon and Green, 2005).

Like Barnes (1976) and his colleagues (Barnes and Todd, 1977, 1995), our approach is grounded in anthropological and discourse perspectives that seek to make visible what is happening in classrooms, how classroom life is socially constructed in and through the discourse-in-use, and how individuals as well as the collective construct opportunities for learning, and social and academic identities (see also, Castanheira, 2004; Bloome et al., 2005). In this way, we seek to identify how common knowledge (Edwards and Mercer, 1987; Mercer and Dawes, Chapter 4, this volume) is constructed, and how common tasks are taken up uncommonly, by small groups or individuals, thus creating different opportunities for learning (as explained, for example, in Kelly et al., 2001).

Also like Barnes, we ask a complex question that makes the situated nature of language and learning relationships visible: who can say or do what, when and where, to and with whom, under what conditions, in what ways, for what purpose(s), with what outcomes and consequences for the collective (the class) as well as for individuals-within-the-class? These questions enable us to explore how members of a class, acting as a culture-in-the-making, construct patterned ways of perceiving, believing, acting and evaluating that constitute the developing culture of the classroom, or what Barnes (1969) called a 'social microcosm'.

In taking this approach, we enter the class prior to the first day to explore how the teacher begins physically structuring the space for the class. We begin to record systematically, using video and fieldnotes, the developing collective on the first day of school, as students enter the class and learn where to sit and what to do in the class. To explore how a community of the classroom is formulated and (re)formulated within and across events on the first day of school, we videotape the whole day (including recess or other breaks). We then follow the developing class for the first three weeks of school, recording every day. After this period, we select key cycles of activity to follow across the school year (Green and Meyer, 1991). As part of this corpus, we, like Barnes and his colleagues (e.g., 1969; 1990), collect the work produced and other relevant artifacts.

This process then provides a broad language context that we then explore to make visible how – in and through the moment-by-moment and over time interactions between the teacher with students and students with others – the class constructs patterned ways of knowing, being and doing. In this way, we explore what counts as common knowledge in particular classrooms, what knowledge counts, and how this knowledge is constructed in and through the roles and relationships, norms and expectations, and rights and obligations constructed by members.

The following excerpt is from a (1995) essay written by Arturo, a fifth grade student (age 10), in a bilingual class taught by a co-author of this chapter, and it represents what we (teachers, students, and researchers) have come to understand about student knowledge of the language of the classroom. (Note that in this excerpt, by 'Tower community' Arturo means his classroom.)

> In our Tower community, we have our own language as well as the languages we bring from outside (like Spanish and English) which helped us make our own language. So, for example, someone that is not from our classroom community would not understand what insider, outsider, think twice, notetaking/notemaking, literature log and learning log mean. If Ms Yeager says we are going to 'make a sand-wich', the people from another class or room would think that we were going to make a sandwich to eat. Of course we aren't, but that is part of our common language …
>
> … These words are all part of the common Tower community lan-guage and if someone new were to come in, we would have to explain how we got them and what they mean. We also would tell them that we got this language by reports, information, investigations, and what we do and learn in our Tower community.

In writing about his community in this way, Arturo, drawing on his work as an ethnographer in his classroom, makes visible that he understands the situated nature of the language of their classroom, and how this language is constitutive of, and constituted by, the learning situations constructed by members of the class. He also recognises how this language differs from the language they bring from other contexts.

In the next section, we illustrate how our ethnographic perspective provides a language and lens for exploring the language of the class-room. The focus of this analysis will be an exploration of the nature of dialogue and writing in a fifth grade classroom. The analysis of dialogue will focus on how the teacher's use of dialogue and writing created opportunities for Jared (age 10) to learn the meaning of, and process involved in, taking a point of view. Through this analysis, we introduce Interactional Ethnography as a *logic of inquiry* that guides our search for evidence of insider knowledge. This approach brings together theories of culture, ethnography and discourse-in-use to cre-ate systematic ways of exploring how, through language as academic and social action, teachers and students can jointly construct a com-municative system, through which they can talk texts and learning processes into being across times and events.

For each phase of Jared's journey, we will draw on conceptual arguments about the relationship of learning and language that Douglas Barnes provides in his chapter in this volume to frame our analysis. Our purpose in taking this integrative and reflexive stance to presenting interactional ethnography as a logic of inquiry is to make visible how reflexivity at the level of theory adds to the expressive potential (Strike, 1974, 1989) of the language of our programme of research, and to provide evidence of the importance of the constructs that guide each analysis. This latter process is what policy makers call *proof of concept*, or in this case evidence of learning in and through the language of the classroom. In this way, we will seek to demonstrate how an integrated body of work on the language of the classroom can provide a richer language than any one programme of research can, for teachers, students and researchers to explore, take up and use.

Dialogue as a rich point for learning: locating an analytic anchor

In initiating our analysis of Jared's journey, our first challenge was to locate a *point of contact* (Barnes and Todd, 1977, building on Bakhtin, 1986) in which dialogue was central to a conversation between the teacher and Jared. The dialogue we selected was identified in a previous analysis (Putney et al., 2000) as a place in which Jared approached the teacher to request help on a task involving point of view. This text, as we show in subsequent sections, became an analytic anchor for identifying the roots of the work represented in this dialogue and related texts across the school year.

Framing this temporal analysis is Barnes's (this volume) argument that:

> Most learning does not happen suddenly. We do not one moment fail to understand something, and then the next moment grasp it entirely ... most of our systems of ideas – call them schemes, frames, models, or concepts – go through a history of development in our minds, some of them changing continually throughout our lives. (Barnes, this volume, p. 4)

This argument introduces two issues we examined in Jared's journey to learning point of view. The first is not something that happens at an isolated point in time but rather is part of a system of ideas. Applied to the present analysis, this statement means that we need to examine how the participants in the dialogue signal to each other what ideas are part of the present event and exploration. Second, any idea has a history. Applying this to the present analysis involved examining how a teacher (re)formulated a history of ideas and events that Jared needed to revisit in order to clarify and (re)formulate his understanding of point of view.

However, before presenting our analysis of these issues, we will present a brief discussion of three conceptual arguments that are part of our orienting framework and how it shapes the approach that we took to analysis of the dialogue as an anchor event. Like Barnes, we understand that students are not passive but rather have agency that shapes what they elect to do and display in classrooms. Thus in analysing Jared's journey, we examine Jared's agency in learning point of view, and how the opportunities for exploring point of view as everyday practice in his classroom and as academic content supported his take up and use of point of view across times and events. In this way, we will make visible how learning events are progressively consequential for students as they develop both a history of ideas and a history of learning processes (Yeager, 1999).

The second conceptual argument that we drew on in this analysis is the view of intertextuality as socially constructed and signalled in the language of the classroom. Bloome and his colleagues (e.g. Bloome and Egan-Robertson, 1993) argue that people in interactions propose, recognise and acknowledge intertextual relationships that are socially, and academically, significant to the participants (see also Floriani, 1993; Heras, 1993). This conceptualisation of intertextuality as socially and discursively accomplished framed our analysis of the talk between Jared and his teacher. As we will show, the teacher proposed references to present and past actions Jared had taken, information he had gained, or contexts that he could revisit to use as a resource for his present exploration. Thus, analysing the developing dialogue for references to intertextual ties became a key way of examining dialogue between Jared and his teacher.

The third theoretical argument is the concept of *rich points* proposed by anthropologist Michael Agar (1994). Agar argues that when something does not go as expected in discourse or in the events of everyday life, a potential *rich point* is constructed. He argues that a rich point is a place where *culture happens*. That is, a frame clash can become a rich point for developing cultural knowledge, when one or more actors in the event pauses to explore what is happening and to consider what they need to understand in order to participate in culturally appropriate ways. This concept provided a way of understanding the processes as well as the meanings that Jared needed to (re)examine. In initiating his dialogue, he states, *I don't understand. Can you explain what you mean about looking at things from a different angle?* In this statement, he is not requesting a definition of point of view, but rather how to engage in a cultural practice – *looking at things from a different angle.*

Dialogue as a rich point for Jared, his teacher, and the researchers

These three constructs – rich points, intertextuality, and student and teacher agency – frame our exploration of dialogue and how it afforded both Jared and his teacher opportunities for constructing a dialogic text and for (re)formulating earlier texts in support of Jared's exploration of point of view. As indicated in Table 7.1 on page 122, we analysed textual, intertextual and exploratory work on a turn-by-turn basis. For each turn at talk, we examined what was being proposed, in what ways, for what purposes, and making what visible. To examine what the outcomes of this process were for both Jared and his teacher, we then examined what each took up and what actions they consequently took in formulating their responses across turns. To examine the consequences for Jared, whether he gained the insights he requested and what the teacher (T) saw him as needing, we then explored the progression of ideas, the local history of ideas, that the teacher supported Jared (J) in exploring.

As indicated in the column entitled, *Textual/Intertextual and Exploratory Work*, the way in which the teacher took up Jared's question involved them both in a discursive journey through time to locate and revisit *hands-on experiences* (Barnes's term, this volume) that Jared had for learning point of view: the first day of school, where the camera was pointed, and whether or not Jared could be seen from where the camera was pointed. In and through this dialogue, as the analysis of column 3 shows, Jared and the teacher brought the past into the present to create a web of intertextual relationships to anchor Jared's request for help.

Through this approach, the teacher helped *to make present* to Jared a range of historical texts that he could (re)visit, (re)examine, (re)think, and use to (re)formulate his understanding of the current

Table 7.1   Dialogue initiated by Jared with his teacher, October 1994

Actor	Dialogue	Textual/Intertextual and Exploratory Work
J:	I don't understand. Can you explain what you mean about looking at things from a different angle?	• Teacher's talk 'looking at things from a different angle' as text.
T:	Well, remember the video of our first day that we observed? We were the ethnographers then.	• Past actions from first day as text. • First day video as text. • Point of view as ethnographers.
J:	OK	
T:	What were you able to see?	• Memory of events as text.
J:	S and V and N moving around, changing tables ...	• Actions of everyday actors as text. • Class discussion as text.
T:	Now, if someone watching that video who wasn't here the first day wanted to know if you were in the class, would they be able to tell?	• Point of view of outsider. • Needing to use insider knowledge. • Teacher leading inquiry.
J:	Not really.	• Memory as insider.
T:	Why?	• Leading inquiry.
J:	Because of where the camera was pointed.	• Seeing through camera angle as text.
T:	Exactly. From the angle of the camera, there were things you could observe and see and things you could not see and what you couldn't see was maybe as important as what you could see.	• Point of view as the relationship between the camera angle, what can be seen or not seen. • actions of observer as text. • strategy that text does not represent the whole.
J:	OK. I get it.	• further internalising.
T:	So, you know, you have to position our scientist or ethnographer ...	• future referent of positioning to illustrate point of view.
J:	So he's looking at it from a certain angle, probably.	• Current dialogue using as text.
T:	You've got it.	• Confirming Jared's understanding of social and academic practices as well as the concept.

talk and the more complex learning process of using and taking up point of view. In creating this opportunity the teacher made visible what is often invisible in the academic work of the class, how the past history and activity of the class can become a resource for academic learning in future tasks. In creating a language of textual and intertextual relationships, Jared and the teacher jointly (re)constructed this point in time, creating an opportunity for learning about Jared's understanding of point of view. In this way, the teacher constructed an opportunity for Jared to present his understandings not as a finished text but as a work in progress.

Through dialogue, therefore, she enabled Jared to make links between the current task and the work he had previously done related to point of view. This brief analysis also provides evidence of Barnes's argument that:

> When learners 'construct' meanings, they are manipulating what is already available to them from various sources, exploring its possibilities, and seeing what can and cannot be done with it. (this volume, p. 9)

This argument summarises what was happening in and through the dialogue of Jared and his teacher. Although this argument is often framed for discussions among students, the dialogue between the teacher and Jared demonstrates how the teacher's use of dialogue enabled Jared to explore the possibilities of using past events and the history of ideas present in these events to (re)construct meaning. Thus, the teacher's use of a discourse about classroom life can be viewed as an explicit text for meaning construction in current events.

Exploring the roots of point of view: analysis of the first day

In the analysis, we examine how the ways in which the teacher constructs the events of life on the first day initiate a set of cultural processes, practices and texts that afford members opportunities to construct what Barnes might call 'a new model or scheme'. He argues that, 'each new model or scheme potentially changes how we experience some aspect of the world, and therefore how we act on it' (this volume, p. 3).

Our purpose in analysing the first day was to examine how its events and actions shaped ways of acting on the language and world under construction in the classroom. In this way we examined the roots of the model that we began to uncover in the dialogue between Jared and his teacher. Furthermore, in exploring what types of actions were taken, what practices were initiated, and what texts were produced and used, we can show how the teacher began structuring communicative and learning processes that formed an intertextual web of life on this morning. In this way, we may explore Barnes's argument that 'The communication system that a teacher sets up in a lesson shapes the roles that the pupils can play, and goes some distance in determining the kinds of learning that they engage in' (this volume, p. 2).

As illustrated in Table 7.2, to explore what members were structuring and to identify what was happening at different levels of the time scale, we used particular forms of language to (re)present the work of the members (Baker and Green, 2007). This table represents an *event map* of the day across multiple time scales (Green and Meyer, 1991). Each column of this map (re)presents a particular dimension of the processes of joint construction that we identified. As indicated in column 2, the Literate Actions column, the actions and phases of activity were (re)presented as present continuous verbs. In this way, we made visible the dynamic and developing sense of work within and across events, rather than making each an object, by transforming actions into nouns (thus drawing on the work of Bloome et al., 2005). The third column provides an analysis of texts produced and used on this day.

Through these representations and maps, we are able to compare and contrast what was made present to students, in what ways, and for what purposes. This form of mapping makes visible that Jared had, from the first moments of his class, multiple and varied opportunities to explore point of view, to participate in learning from and with others, and to explore multiple sources of information that could be used in his class to represent self in different groups (table groups and whole class), as well as to explore others in the class as texts (e.g., the Name Game). This table, therefore, provides a way of making visible how the communicative system that the teacher initiated was tied to particular events and how, in turn, the events made available a particular set of practices, a communicative repertoire, and a developing language of the classroom tied to situated events being constructed.

Through this brief analysis, we were able to make visible a *sketch map* of the practices she used to create the opportunities for learning the *ground rules* (Barnes, 1976; see also Mercer and Dawes, Chapter 4 this volume) of the class. Additionally, by tying this analysis to the dialogue between the teacher and Jared, we were able to identify how dialogue and writing were a resource used throughout this day. Furthermore, the analysis showed and made visible the range of texts – oral, visual (video) and written – that had the potential to become

Table 7.2 Map of the events constructed through the actions of members on the first morning

Events and Phases of Activity	Literate and Social Actions and Practices	Texts Produced and Used
8:30 School begins Initiating Community * arriving, forming unofficial table groups and making name tiles	* selecting name cards * choosing where to sit in table groups * drawing on name tile * talking with table group members * introducing chime as signal * explaining active listening * introducing adults in community • student teacher, teacher aide, university ethnographers	* name cards * positioning self at a table * decorated name card (for quilt) * student–student interpersonal * chime as signal-word on whiteboard * the look of listening * roles of adults as text * study of own class * definition of historical self
* establishing roles and relationships, norms and expectations	* introducing ethnography as community practice * discussing life in prior communities * defining ways of living in Tower community * explaining insider knowledge as member of McKinley community	* definition of Tower member * definition of school member
Name Game activity	* introducing Name Game procedures * selecting adjective to represent self * introducing self to table group * introducing self to whole group * naming members of the class who have been introduced	* descriptors for teacher on whiteboard in English and Spanish * descriptor of self (Choice of Language) * introducing self – adjective + name (choice of Language) * (re)stating names of students who have already introduced self – adjective + name (use of both languages)
Watermelon Project * utilising Learning logs	* defining mathematicians * introducing how to use name first part of learning log – mathematics	* definition of student mathematicians * learning logs (spiral notebooks) as class textbook

(Continued)

Table 7.2   (Continued)

Events and Phases of Activity	Literate and Social Actions and Practices	Texts Produced and Used
	10:50 Recess (20 minutes)	
Watermelon Project * transitioning to problem	* explaining tradition of watermelons * formulating questions as part of investigating * asking particular question to be answered * making a guess * making an estimate, collecting data * revising the estimate from data collection * explicating the process used so far	* teacher narrative on personal tradition: linking local class to previous classes * question written in learning Logs * question as problem to be solved * entry in learning logs * entry in learning logs * entry in learning logs * chart on whiteboard to be copied
	12:15: Lunch and play period (50 minutes)	

academically and socially significant resources for future work, as the dialogue showed.

Evidence of learning point of view: Jared's North Carolina essay

In this final section, we present an essay that we identified in March of the school year. In this essay Jared showed how he took up and used point of view for academic work. He also made clear how point of view became an academic resource in writing social science. Thus, this essay provides further evidence of the argument by Douglas Barnes that:

> When learners 'construct' meanings, they are manipulating what is already available to them from various sources, exploring its possibilities, and seeing what can and cannot be done with it. (this volume, p. 9)

Therefore, in this essay Jared demonstrates how he used the historical web of ideas to decide how to construct his essay as well as what to include.

North Carolina Essay, Colony Project

March 1994

I am a Native American from the Cherokee living in the Southeast. When the English came, we knew they had more power than us, so we thought that maybe if we did things like them, they would let us stay. We developed our own republic. We had writing and our own newspaper. It really was our land before they came. After a long time, they wanted us to pay taxes to them, but we didn't. Then in the 1830s, the Americans came and walked my descendants from North Carolina to the plains. A lot of us died during the walk. We started out as one colony and in 1691, we divided into two colonies.

I am an Englishman who went to North Carolina. When we got there, there were Indians on our land. We ignored them for a while. Then we decided to have them as slaves or pay taxes. They didn't want to do either. Years later, the Americans made them walk from North Carolina and Georgia to the plains. People died but they didn't mean for anyone to die.

We settled in the Carolinas in 1652. Our King, King Charles II, later sent an army to take it over. North Carolina was founded so England could have the three expensive things: wine, silk, and olive oil. We grew rice and indigo in the Carolinas to trade and sell. When the Indians wouldn't do the work, we brought in slaves from Africa.

As Jared's essay shows, he presented the history of North Carolina by not using the traditional nation building arguments (see Van Sledright, 2008), but rather in a way that described different historical realities and their interactions. He presented the history of the Cherokee in relationship to colonial America and colonial North Carolina in relationship to England. In this essay, not only does he shift across the points of view of different people, he also inscribes multiple historical timelines. Furthermore, in highlighting these different points of view, Jared used a narrative structure that breaks with the traditional five-paragraph essay. In creating an essay that shift points of view in this way, he demonstrates writing processes and practices available to him in this class, and how he adapted them, manipulating them in a creative way, to accomplish his goal of presenting different points of view on the history of what is officially called, in American History textbooks, 'The North Carolina Colony'.

In using his text structure in this way, and by including multiple time scales and multiple angles of vision, Jared provides a presentational text for us to learn more about the language and social microcosm of his class. In this text, our ethnographic records showed that as Jared presented to his class as part of a Colony Project, he contributed to the development of a collective text of the class that led members to identify historical, social, geographic and economic patterns. Thus, through this form of presentational text Jared showed his class (and us as researchers) ways of thinking, working, understanding and representing the learning processes available in his class that supported him in exploring and constructing meanings about what counted as knowledge, as ways of knowing, being and doing academic work, and ways of describing and representing his thinking as a social scientist.

Conclusion

This brief exploration of Jared's journey is not the complete story. In mapping intertextual relationships across time for learning point of view, we point out how dialogue and writing were also to be noted in the dialogues between Jared and his teacher, in the actions taken in the classroom and the language constructed in and through these actions, and in the range of opportunities for writing afforded Jared.

This analysis also explores the juxtaposition of texts from different points in time that members signal are socially and academically significant. Through this analysis, we were able to provide evidence of the constructs that Barnes provided. Thus, as we explored his constructs and how they supply a language or anchor for our analysis of Jared's journey, we provided further evidence that these concepts could be generalised across programmes of research.

The reflexive use of theory in this chapter suggests that the process of analysis through different theoretical lenses, whether by teachers or by researchers, has the potential for creating a common interpretation of the language of the classroom. We believe that by creating a common language that is generalisable across educational contexts, we can provide policy makers, teachers and researchers with systematic and empirical ways of gaining richer and more robust evidence of the consequential nature of talk (and writing) in classrooms that will honour the complex work of teachers and students, as they talk texts and learning processes into being.

References

Agar, M. (1994) *Language Shock: Understanding the Culture of Conversation*. New York: Perennial (Harper Collins).

Baker, W.D. and Green, J. (2007) 'Limits to certainty in interpreting video data: interactional ethnography and disciplinary knowledge', *Pedagogies*, 2 (3).

Bakhtin, M. (1986) *Speech Genres and Other Late Essays*. Austin, TX: University of Texas Press.

Barnes, D. (1969) 'Language in the secondary classroom', in D. Barnes, J. Britton and H. Rosen (eds), *Language, the Learner and the School*. Harmondsworth: Penguin.

Barnes, D. (1976) *From Communication to Curriculum*. Harmondsworth: Penguin.

Barnes, D. and Todd, F. (1977) *Communication and Learning in Small Groups*. Abingdon: Routledge and Kegan Paul.

Barnes, D. and Todd, F. (1995) *Communication and Learning Revisited: Making Meaning Through Talk*. London: Boynton/Cook.

Barnes, D., Britton, J. and Rosen, H. (1969) *Language, the Learner, and the School*. (first edition). Harmondsworth: Penguin.

Barnes, D., Britton, J. and Torbe, M. (1990) *Language, the Learner and the School* (fourth edition). Portsmouth, NH: Heinemann.

Bloome, D. and Egan-Robertson, A. (1993) 'The social construction of intertextuality in classroom reading and writing lessons', *Reading Research Quarterly*, 28 (4): 305–33.

Bloome, D., Carter, S., Christian, B., Otto, S. and Shuart-Faris, N. (2005) *Discourse Analysis and the Study of Classroom Language and Literacy Events: A Microethnographic Approach*. Mahwah, NJ: Erlbaum Associates.

Castanheira, M.L. (2004). Aprendizagem Contextualizada: discurso e inclusão na sala de aula. Belo Horizonte: Ceale; Autêntica.

Dixon and Green, 2005; Dixon, C. & Green, J. (2005). Studying the discursive construction of texts in classrooms through interactional ethnography. In R. Beach; J.L. Green; M. Kamil & T. Shanahan (eds), Multidisciplinary perspectives on literacy research. Cresshill, NJ: Hampton Press, 349–90.

Edwards, D. and Mercer, N. (1987) *Common Knowledge: The Development of Understanding in the Classroom*. New York: Routledge.

Floriani, A. (1993) 'Negotiating what counts: roles and relationships, content and meaning, texts and context', *Linguistics and Education*, 5 (3 and 4). Norwood, NJ: Ablex: 241–74.

Green, J. and Dixon, C. (1993) 'Talking knowledge into being: discursive and social practices in classrooms', *Linguistics and Education*, 5 (3 and 4): 231–9.

Green, J. and Meyer, L.A. (1991) 'The embeddedness of reading in classroom life: reading as a situated process', in C. Baker and A. Luke (eds), *Towards a Critical Sociology of Reading Pedagogy*. Amsterdam: John Benjamins. pp. 141–60.

Heras, A.I. (1993) 'The construction of understanding in a sixth grade bilingual classroom', *Linguistics and Education*, 5 (3 and 4). Norwood, NJ: Ablex. pp. 275–99.

Kelly, G.J., Crawford, T., & Green, J. (2001). Common tasks and uncommon knowledge: Dissenting voices in the discursive construction of physics across small laboratory groups. *Lingustics and* Education, 12(2), 135–74.

Putney, L., Green, J., Dixon, C., Durán, R. and Yeager, B. (2000) 'Consequential progressions: exploring collective–individual development in a bilingual classroom', in C. Lee and P. Smagorinsky (eds), *Vygotskian Perspectives on Literacy Research.* Cambridge: Cambridge University Press.

Santa Barbara Classroom Discourse Group (1992a) 'Constructing literacy in classrooms: literate action as social accomplishment', in H. Marshall (ed.), *Redefining Student Learning: Roots of Educational Restructuring.* Norwood, NJ: Ablex. pp. 119–50.

Santa Barbara Classroom Discourse Group (1992b) 'Do you see what we see? The eferential and intertextual nature of classroom life', *Journal of Classroom Interaction, 27* (2): 29–36.

Strike, K. (1974) 'On the expressive potential of behaviorist language', *American Educational Research Journal,* 11 (2): 103–20.

Strike, K. (1989) *Liberal Justice and the Marxist Critique of Education.* New York: Routledge.

VanSledright, B. (2008). Narratives of Nation-State, Historical Knowledge, and School History Education. In G. Kelly, A. Luke, and J. Green (eds), *Review of Research in Education,* 32, 109–46.

Yeager, B. (1999) 'Constructing a community of inquirers', *Primary Voices K-6,* 7: 337–52.

Yeager, B., Floriani, A. and Green, J. (1998) 'Learning to see learning in the classroom: developing an ethnographic perspective', in A. Egan-Robertson and D. Bloome (eds), *Students As Researchers Of Culture And Language In Their Own Communities.* New Jersey: Hampton Press. pp. 115–39.

Note

This chapter contains contributions from members of the Santa Barbara classroom Discourse Group, University of California.

Teachers' Use of Feedback in Whole-class and Group-based Talk

Frank Hardman

Summary

In this chapter, Frank Hardman argues that international research shows that it is important that teachers use classroom dialogue to encourage students' active participation and to provide them with constructive feedback. This requires teachers to use a variety of strategies for interacting with their students, and especially for using questions in strategic ways. However, observational research also shows that this importance is not reflected by practice in most class-rooms, where the questions asked by teachers still seem to be designed to elicit only brief 'right answers' and where teachers' eval-uations of those answers provide little in the way of useful, formative assessment. Hardman argues for the need for teacher training on the use of questions and a greater understanding of how feedback can support learning and shape the development of students' thinking.

For Discussion

1 What is meant by a 'recitation script', and why is Hardman critical of teachers' dependence on it?
2 How have Vygotsky and Bakhtin contributed to present-day understanding of the role of talk in teaching and learning?

(Continued)

(Continued)

3   In your experience, how common is it for teachers to ask open questions, and to sustain extended dialogue with students?

4   How might a teacher use questions to 'open up' classroom dialogue and so help students take a more active role in their learning?

5   What implications are there here for teachers' training and professional development?

Recent research into formative assessment emphasises the power of feedback in enhancing the teaching and learning process (Black and Wiliam, 1998; Black et al., 2003). Feedback is found to be particularly powerful when it is used by teachers to adapt their teaching to the learning needs of students, and when it focuses on the qualities of student work and offers guidance on what can be done to bring about improvements. Such teacher feedback can be in both spoken and written forms. In emphasising the power of feedback in enhancing the learning and teaching process, however, Black et al. (2003) recognise that there need to be fundamental changes to underlying pedagogic practices so that students play a more active part in their own learning.

The focus of this chapter is on effective oral feedback in activities where students are able to actively participate in their own learning and communicate their evolving understanding in spoken forms in group-based, whole-class and one-to-one interactions. In it I will discuss the centrality of talk in the learning process and the extent to which teachers can enhance student learning through questioning and feedback which asks students to expand on their thinking, justify or clarify their opinions, or make connections to their own experiences. It will also address how the professional development needs of teachers can be met so as to enhance the quality of oral feedback in the classroom.

The chapter draws on my research into the power of talk to shape student thinking and to secure their engagement, learning and understanding in classroom study. My line of enquiry began in the UK and covered various phases of education (Edwards et al., 1997; Hardman and Leat, 1998; Hardman and Williamson, 1998; Hardman and Mroz, 1999; Mroz et al., 2000; Hardman et al., 2003; Hardman et al., 2005; Smith et al., 2004; Smith et al., 2006; Smith et al., 2007). Three national UK studies, using both quantitative and qualitative approaches to study classroom interaction and discourse at a macro and micro level, yielded somewhat depressing findings about the character of classroom talk from primary school through to post-16 education. More recently, my research has been extended into an international context to explore the relevance of effective oral feedback in the developing world, particularly in Kenya and Nigeria (Ackers and Hardman, 2001; Pontefract and Hardman, 2005; Abd-Kadir and Hardman, 2007; Hardman et al., 2007; Hardman et al., 2008; Hardman et al., in press). From these studies, it was found that one kind of talk predominates: the so-called 'recitation script' of closed teacher questions, brief student answers and minimal feedback which requires students to report someone else's thinking rather than think for themselves, and to be evaluated on their compliance in doing so.

From this work there has developed the concept of a dialogic pedagogy where teachers are helped to break out of the limitations of the recitation script through higher order questioning and feedback strategies which promote a range of alternative discourse strategies. Alexander (2004) has described the essential features of 'dialogic talk' as being collective (teachers and students address the learning task together), reciprocal (teachers and students listen to each other to share ideas and consider alternative viewpoints), supportive (students articulate their ideas freely without fear of embarrassment over 'wrong' answers and support each other to reach common understandings), cumulative (teachers and students build on their own and each other's ideas to chain them into coherent lines of thinking and enquiry), and purposeful (teachers plan and facilitate dialogic teaching with educational goals in mind). Most importantly, it can take place in whole-class, group-based and individual interactions between teachers and students.

The centrality of talk in learning

Helping students to become more adept at using language is seen as one of the major goals of education in order that they can express their thoughts and engage with others in joint intellectual activity to develop their communication skills and to advance their individual capacity for productive, rational and reflective thinking. The guided co-construction of knowledge, in which a tutor talks with students in whole-class, group and individual settings to guide their thinking, is therefore seen as being central to the educational process (Hardman,

2007). In this theory of learning, teachers and learners are regarded as active participants in the construction of knowledge on the basis of ideas and experiences contributed by students as well as by their teacher (Wells, 1999; Mercer, 2000).

As Douglas Barnes points out in his chapter on exploratory talk, Vygotsky was one of the first psychologists to acknowledge the role of talk in organising learners' understanding of the world (see Chapter 1, this volume). In his book *Thought and Language*, first published in Russia in the 1930s and translated into English in 1962, Vygotsky suggested that using language to communicate helps in the development of new ways of thinking: what children learn from their 'inter-mental' experience (communication between minds through social interaction) shapes their 'intra-mental' activity (the way they think as individuals). More importantly, Vygotsky argued that the greatest influence on the development of thinking would come from the interaction between a learner and a more knowledgeable, supportive member of a community, such as a parent or teacher. In what became known as the 'zone of proximal development' – the zone between what a learner can do unaided and can manage with expert assistance – social interaction was seen as being central to instruction. A similar emphasis on the social origins of the individual's language repertoire is found in the work of the Russian philosopher Bakhtin whose work, like Vygotsky's, was published in the 1920s and 30s but was not translated into English until the 1960s (Holquist, 1990). Bakhtin argued that dialogue pervades all spoken and written discourse and is essential where meanings are not fixed or absolute. It is therefore central to educational discourse and learning because of the need to consider alternative frames of reference.

Out of the work of these early theorists developed the social constructivist view of learning which suggests that classroom discourse is not effective unless students play an active part in their learning through exploratory forms of talk. This view of learning suggests that it does not take place through the addition of discrete facts to an existing store of knowledge, but when new information, experiences and ways of understanding are related to an existing understanding of the matter in hand. One of the most important ways of working on this understanding is through talk, particularly where students are given the opportunity to assume greater control over their own learning by initiating ideas and responses. In this way, they can contribute to the shaping of the verbal agenda and introduce alternative frames of reference which are open to negotiation and where the criteria of relevance are not imposed. The social constructivist theory of learning therefore questions the value of the linguistic and cognitive demands made on students within the traditional whole-class teaching format, where they are mainly expected to be passive and to recall, when asked, what they have learned and to report other people's thinking.

In the development of a social constructivist view of learning, the notion of teaching as 'transmission', in which knowledge is presented as closed, authoritative and immutable rather than open to discussion and interpretation, was challenged. Drawing upon insights from the work of the early dialogic theorists, Barnes, Britton and Rosen (1969) developed a critical and cross-curricular analysis of what they saw as teachers' overwhelming use of transmissional forms of teaching. Rather than seeing talk in learning as a linear process, they argued it should be a reciprocal process in which ideas are discussed between student and teacher so as to take thinking forward.

Teacher questions

In an attempt to open up classroom discourse and encourage greater participation, research has focussed on the promotion of 'higher-order' questioning techniques to promote reflection, self-examination and enquiry through the use of 'open' questions which invite students to speculate, hypothesise, reason, evaluate and to consider a range of possible answers (see, for example, Brown and Wragg, 1993). However, the use of questions in the classroom as a strategy for guiding the co-construction of knowledge was strongly challenged by empirical evidence which showed the overwhelming reliance of teachers on 'closed' factual questions in which students provide the 'right' answer as defined by the teacher (Wood, 1992; Dillon, 1994; Galton et al., 1980, 1999).

Challenging the notion that teachers can be trained to ask better questions, Dillon (1994) argues that a high level question might be said to express a high level of thinking on the part of the teacher but it does not necessarily cause it in the respondent. He suggests that discussion usually begins with a problem in which all the participants share some perplexity giving rise to genuine questions; however, teachers are rarely perplexed about the questions they ask, as they typically know the answers, so there is little opportunity for sharing the question and therefore stimulating either teacher or student thought. Similarly, Galton et al. (1999) classified teacher questions in terms of how they react to student answers rather than the apparent intentions of the teacher: only if the teacher accepted more than one answer to a question would it be judged as 'open' rather than 'closed'.

In order for teachers to be more effective in opening up classroom talk to students, a range of alternatives to teacher questions has been suggested which include the use of provocative, open-ended statements, encouraging students to ask their own questions and maintaining silence so that they have thinking time before they respond (Edwards, 1992; Dillon, 1994). Such alternatives to teacher questions will also lead, as will be discussed in the next session, to a shift in emphasis in the way teachers react in their feedback to student responses.

The difficulty of managing the turn-taking of a large numbers of students in whole-class talk has also led to the questioning of the effectiveness of teacher questioning and the development of group-based learning. For example, Barnes and Todd (1977) went on to explore the promotion of student talk through the use of collaborative group work as a way of 'decentralising' classroom communication and allowing for alternative frames of reference to be explored. In discussing the features of group work where students are encouraged to explore meanings collaboratively, Barnes and Todd (1995) pointed out the clear differences in discourse structure between this and a whole-class question and answer routine. Because the absence of the teacher means there is no authoritative figure to dominate the discourse, there are no clearly marked asymmetrical relationships, and the consequent lack of pre-allocated rights makes it necessary for the students to negotiate the terms of their interaction as they go along. The patterns of interaction are therefore strikingly different from the kinds of discourse associated with the whole-class, transmission model of teaching. In this way, as Mercer (1995) suggests, students can share in and practise forms of academic discourse of the classroom normally inhabited by the teacher: that is, sharing, comparing, contrasting and arguing from different perspectives, providing opportunities for instructional conversation or the shared construction or negotiation of meaning. Therefore in group or paired work, students are given more opportunities to develop linguistically and cognitively.

The patterning of teacher–student interaction

Work on the linguistic patterning of teacher–student interaction by Sinclair and Coulthard (1975) first revealed the initiation–response-feedback (IRF) exchange as being central to teacher/student interaction in English primary classrooms. They identified that a teaching exchange consists of three moves: an *initiation*, usually in the form of a teacher question, a *response* in which a student attempts to answer the question, and a *follow-up* move, in which the teacher provides some form of feedback. While they found teacher follow-up was very often in the form of an evaluation to a student's response, teachers sometimes used comments which exemplified, expanded, justified or added additional information to student responses. Sinclair and Coulthard also identified a *re-initiation* as a probing move where if a teacher received a wrong answer s/he could stay with the same child to bring him/her round to the right answer.

The ubiquity of the three-part exchange structure was very evident in my study of the impact of the national strategies on the teaching of literacy and numeracy in primary classrooms in England (Mroz et al., 2000; Hardman et al., 2003; Smith et al., 2004; Hardman et al., 2005; Smith et al., 2006; Smith et al., 2007). The following extract, taken from a Year 5 literacy lesson class, is typical of the discourse style used by teachers when interacting with students. Here the teacher is exploring various grammatical features in a newspaper report: (the *moves* (Initiation, Response, Feedback) make up the three-part teaching exchange and which in turn are made up of *acts*; ch = teacher check; cl = clue; com = teacher comment; d = teacher direct; e = teacher evaluation; el = teacher question; i = teacher inform; n = nomination; p = prompt; rep = reply; s = starter. Boundaries indicated by a marker (m) and/or meta-statement (ms) show a change in lesson topic; T = teacher; B = boy; G = girl).

Exchanges				Moves	Acts
Teaching	T	ok		I	m
		Looking at the text now I want you please	I	s
		to tell me what tense the first paragraph		
		is in what tense the first paragraph is in.		el
2	G	The past tense.		R	rep
3	T	Yes it's in the past tense.		F	e
4	T	How do you know it's in the past tense?	I	el

5	G	Because it says August 1990.	R	rep
6	T	You know by the date it's in the past tense	F	e
7	T	but you know by something else you know you know by the doing words in the text that change.	I	s
		What's a doing word?		el
		What do we call a doing word, David?		n
8	B	A verb.	R	rep
9	T	A verb good.	F	e
10	T	Will you give me one verb please out of this first paragraph.	I	s
		Find one verb in this paragraph,		el
		Stephen.		n
11	B	Rescued.	R	r
12	T	Rescued excellent excellent and that's in the past tense.	F	e com
13	T	Does the tense change when it comes to the next paragraph?	I	s
		Remember it's the verb that will tell you.		cl
		Skim, find the verbs that was the past that happened before this is now it's happening now.		i
		Does the verb change Julie?		n/el
14	G	It's the present.	R	rep
15	T	It's the present tense of the verb.	F	e
16	T	Can anybody find me one verb in there in the present tense?	I	s
		Skim down, see if you can find a verb in the tense.		e l
		Lucy.		n
17	G	Catch.	R	rep
18	T	Catch right.	F	e

This section illustrates clearly the teacher's pervasive use of the three-part exchange and the elaborate nature of many of her sequences of elicits which are chained together to form a lengthy transaction. The extract also illustrates how the teacher often uses *starter* acts (Turns 1, 7, 10, 13, 16) as a matter of routine in opening moves. These are similar in function to what Edwards and Mercer (1987) call 'cued elicitations', where she provides advance warning that a question is imminent and also provides some clues as to how to answer it.

We can in addition see the teacher 'reformulate' a question (Turn 7) in the sequence in an attempt to arrive at the answer she desires, by simplifying and building into its restatement some of the information needed for the acceptable answer and where the ingredients of an appropriate answer might lie. It shows the way in which teacher-directed talk of this kind creates the impression of knowledge and understanding being elicited from the students rather than being imposed by the teacher. The extract also reveals the rapid pace of the teacher's questioning and the predictable sequence of recitation. There is a large amount of teacher elaboration through the use of *starters* and the rephrasing of questions in contrast to the brief responses expected from the students which show a high incidence of simple recall. The student responses are evaluated and commented on by the teacher who has the right to determine what is relevant within her pedagogic agenda.

My research in primary classrooms in Kenya and Nigeria also shows that teacher–student interaction often takes the form of lengthy recitations of question (by the teacher) and answer (by individual students or the whole class) within an IRF structure (Ackers and Hardman, 2001; Pontefract and Hardman, 2005; Abd-Kadir and Hardman, 2007; Hardman et al., 2008). However, the studies also show interesting discourse variations when compared to studies from the developed world, particularly in the use of cued elicitations and the follow-up move of the three-part, IRF structure. One prominent eliciting move was the use of a mid-sentence rise in voice intonation that acted as a teacher elicit designed to get a response from the students during or after an explanation, or following a student response. Usually, the elicitation was in the form of a repetition or completion of a phrase or word. It was often direct and students knew from the intonation of the elicitation whether it required an individual answer or a choral response. This we categorised as a form of cued elicitation and it often functioned as a re-initiation move embedded within a teaching exchange. Such cued elicitations therefore functioned as ritualised participation strategies designed to keep the students involved rather than requiring an answer to a question.

The following extract, taken from a primary Year 6 English lesson taught by a male Nigerian teacher exploring the formation of adjectives from nouns, is typical of the discourse style used by both Nigerian and Kenyan teachers (Re-initiations (R/I) moves are embedded within a teaching exchange and together with the act of cued elicitation (ce) are often designed to elicit a repetition or completion of a phrase or word; ^ indicates rising intonation; T = teacher; B = boy; G = girl; C = choral response).

Exchanges				Moves	Acts
Boundary	T	Now^		I	m
		having identified the adjectives formed from these nouns we now attempt to look at the meanings of the new words that are formed.		ms	
2	T	Are you alright there?		I	ch
3	C	Yes.		R	rep
4	T	We now attempt to look at the meanings of some new words say that are formed for instance when we formed ok say (writes on board).		I	i
		What are the meanings of new words formed? We're trying I mean look at the meanings of new words formed here so that it will guide us as we apply them in sentences.			
5	T	Are you ready there yeah?		I	ch
6	C	Yes.		R	rep
7	T	So now this is (writes on board) we'll look at the words formed and we'll look at their meanings.		I	i
8	T	Are you alright there?		I	ch
9	C	Yes.		R	rep
10	T	For instance I want to talk about the word care talk about the word what.^		I	ce
11	C	Care.		R	rep

12	T	I'll talk about the word careless. Instead we have formed the word careless from the word care so what is the meaning of the word careless to not be careful?	I	i
13	T	Not being what?^	R/I	ce
14	C	Not being careful.	R	rep
15	T	I also talked about harm.	I	i
16	T	All say harm.^	R/I	ce
17	C	Harm.	R	rep
18	T	Harmless.^	R/I	ce
19	C	Harmless.	R	rep
20	T	Harm.^	R/I	ce
21	C	Harmless.	R	rep
22	T	Talk about the word harm–harmless it is formed less we now have the word harmless which means what not being harmful.	I	i
23	T	All say not being harmful.	R/I	ce
24	C	Not being harmful.	R	rep
25	T	Again.	R/I	ce
26	C	Not being harmful.	R	rep
27	T	Yes harmless harmless there's the spelling.	I	s
		Harmless is not being what?^		el
28	C	Harmful.	R	rep

The extract reveals the extent to which the classroom discourse is made up of teacher explanation (Turns 4, 7, 12, 22) and question and answer sequences. Choral responses (Turns 3, 6, 9, 11, 14, 17, 19, 21, 24, 26, 28) are common and often follow the re-initiations (Turns 13, 16, 18, 20, 23, 25) used to reinforce information given by the teacher or elicited from a pupil answer. Pupils often know from the intonation of the first move of an exchange whether it requires an individual answer or a choral response. Because the discourse structure is often made up of a teacher initiation and pupil response, the lack of follow up normally precludes any systematic building upon pupil answers. The structure of the interaction appears highly ritualised and the repertoire is clearly understood by the pupils, hence the low number of teacher directs. The practice of asking pupils to complete a sentence either through a direct repetition of a teacher's explanation or pupil answer, or through omitting the final word, or words, or a combination of both these strategies, was therefore very common.

Teacher use of feedback

While extensive research in the USA by Nystrand et al. (1997) and Cazden (2001) found managing the quality of classroom discourse to be the most important factor if there is to be genuine dialogic teaching, leading to significant gains in learning outcomes, the studies also found that there was a persistence of closed, factual questioning and the low-level evaluation of student responses. For example, in their analysis of more than 200 eighth and ninth-grade English and social studies classes in a variety of schools in the Midwest, Nystrand and his colleagues found that whole-class discussion, in which there is an open exchange of ideas, averaged less than 50 seconds in the eighth grade and less than 15 seconds in the ninth grade. In a quantitative re-analysis of their earlier data using indicators such as open-ended questions, uptake questions (building a student's answer into a subsequent question), student questions, cognitive level and level of evaluation, Nystrand et al. (2003) found that shifts from recitational to dialogic discourse patterns were rare. In the 1,151 instructional episodes that they observed (namely, when a teacher moves on to a new topic) only 66 episodes (6.69 per cent) could be described as being dialogic in nature.

Similarly, my research of the UK's national primary literacy and numeracy strategies revealed that traditional patterns of whole-class interaction have not been dramatically transformed by the strategies (Hardman et al., 2003; Smith et al., 2004; Hardman et al., 2005; Smith et al., 2006; Smith et al., 2007). Using a computerised systematic observation system to analyse video recorded lessons, it was found that in the whole-class section of literacy and numeracy lessons, teachers spent the majority of their time either explaining or using highly structured question and answer sequences. Far from encouraging and extending student contributions to promote higher levels of interaction and cognitive engagement, most of the questions asked were of a low cognitive level designed to funnel student responses towards a required answer. Open questions (designed to elicit more than one answer) made up 10 per cent of the questioning exchanges and 15 per cent of the sample did not ask any such questions. Probing by the teacher – where the teacher stayed with the same students to ask further questions to encourage sustained and extended dialogue occurred – occurred in just over 11 per cent of the questioning exchanges. Uptake questions occurred in only 4 per cent of the teaching exchanges and 43 per cent of the teachers did not use any such moves. Only rarely were teachers' questions used to assist students towards more complete or elaborated ideas. Most of the students' exchanges were very short, lasting on average five seconds, and were limited to three words or less for 70 per cent of the time. It was also very rare for students to initiate the questioning. In studies of teacher–student dialogue in the small-group 'guided' sessions, it was also found that teachers exercised tight control over the parameters of relevance and were reluctant to allow student initiation or modification of the topic (Skidmore et al., 2003; Hardman et al., 2005).

In Kenyan and Nigerian primary classrooms it was found that teacher questions and cued elicitations accounted for nearly 60 per cent of the I-moves followed by teacher informs (38per cent). Student questions were very rare (less than 1per cent). In the R-moves, over 60 per cent of the responses were choral, 21 per cent were answered by boys and 10 per cent by girls. Student demonstration accounted for 3 per cent of the responses and most were carried out by boys. In the F-moves, over 50 per cent of responses received no follow up, particularly when a teacher elicitation called for a choral answer. When it did occur, teachers usually accepted an answer in 25 per cent of the follow-up moves or praised it (14 per cent) often by asking the class to applaud. However, teacher comments on student answers whereby they would rephrase, build or elaborate upon an answer were very rare, accounting for less than 2 per cent of the follow-up moves, as were teacher probes whereby a teacher would stay with a student and ask for further elaboration upon his/her answer (3 per cent). Another dimension used to analyse the student responses was their word length; here the data related to all student responses – that is both choral and individual. It was found in both sets of data that over 90 per cent of responses were three words or less for both choral and individual responses. The analysis of the length of responses therefore suggests students had little opportunity to respond at length to teacher initiations.

My work in the post-16 sector in the UK also revealed that the teaching of students about to embark on university study is dominated by teacher explanation and recitation (Edwards et al., 1997; Hardman and Leat, 1998; Hardman and Williamson, 1998; Hardman and Mroz, 1999). There was an overwhelming predominance of teacher-directed question and answer and presentation, accounting for 63 per cent of the total teaching exchanges in post-16 English lessons. The findings challenged the general assumption about the nature of classroom interaction, where 'good practice' is often conceived of as being a seminar in which the teacher is no more than a leading participant and mediating influence in a process of discovery. Such a notion assumes students have the right to challenge and question as they acquire some of the working practices of the subject and participate in the discourse in preparation for university study. However, student questions accounted for just 4 per cent of the teaching exchanges, suggesting that exploration of a topic through student initiations so as to allow an interchange of ideas was rarely practised. Overall the findings point to the universal nature of teacher-led recitation in both the developed and developing world and suggest the need for an alternative, 'universalistic' pedagogy which emphasises joint teacher–pupil activity and higher order thinking.

How can teacher feedback support learning?

Such findings on the lack of student engagement in classroom talk from both the developed and developing world have led some researchers to call for the demise of the IRF (Lemke, 1990; Wood, 1992). While accepting its pervasiveness, other researchers have argued IRF can be functionally effective, leading to very different levels of student engagement and participation. Mercer (1995), for example, argues that it can be an effective means of monitoring students' knowledge and understanding, guiding their learning and identifying knowledge and experience which are considered educationally significant, thereby promoting academic forms of discourse. Others suggest that the IRF structure can take on a variety of forms and functions leading to different levels of student participation and engagement, particularly through the use that is made of the follow-up move.

Through his comparative research into classroom talk in primary school classrooms in five countries (England, France, India, Russia, USA), Alexander (2000) found that although the IRF exchange is ubiquitous, it is used in different ways to organise the communicative process of teaching and learning. While in most of the classrooms he observed that teachers spoke for the majority of the time, the contribution of the students varied considerably across the different cultures, leading to different levels of student participation and cognitive engagement. In Russian and French classrooms Alexander found it was more common for a teacher to probe a student's response, leading to higher levels of student engagement and longer stretches of discourse conducted through a more formal academic discourse, when compared to British and American classrooms. Alexander suggests that this reflects a commitment in French and Russian schools to collective/public, rather than individualised, learning.

Similarly, Nystrand et al. (1997) found that when teachers paid more attention to the way in which they evaluated student responses there was more 'high-level evaluation' whereby teachers incorporated student answers into subsequent questions. In this process, which they term *uptake*, teacher's questions should be shaped by what immediately preceded them so that they were genuine questions. When such high-level evaluation occurred, the teacher ratified the importance of a student's response and allowed it to modify or affect the course of the discussion in some way, weaving it into the fabric of an unfolding exchange thereby encouraging more student-initiated ideas and responses, and consequently promoting higher-order thinking. Nassaji and Wells (2000) also found that teacher feedback could extend and draw out the significance of the answer. From their research, they advocated that teachers use comments and probing questions to open up the F-move so as to invite further student elaboration and create a more equal mode of participation.

Similar findings also emerged from my own research of UK and African classrooms: when dialogic episodes did occur, teachers opened up space in the classroom discourse by explicitly encouraging students to review one another's contributions. The teachers also encouraged more symmetric interaction by demonstrating reciprocal engagement with student responses through exclamations of interest often combined with statements that related the student's response to their own personal experience or opinion. Some of the teachers also demonstrated a more flexible approach to unpredicted student responses by turning the feedback move into another question and asking for clarification. Such questions were authentic in the sense that they were asking about something genuinely unknown to the teacher, thereby ratifying the importance of the student's original response while also creating an opportunity for the student to expand upon their original response. Other teachers explored student contributions by incorporating them into the immediate discussion or by using them to frame a new topic or exchange.

Enhancing pedagogical practice

It is clear from my review of the research that major challenges have to be overcome if classroom talk is to be transformed from recitation into dialogue so as to promote the guided construction of knowledge between teachers and students. The persistence of teacher-led recitation suggests a need for the exploration and researching of alternative teaching and learning strategies and the introduction of powerful school-based in-service programmes in order to change habitual classroom behaviours and traditional discourse patterns.

In order to enhance classroom practice and promote dialogic forms of talk in the classroom, research into professional learning has started to explore the link between discourse patterns and teachers' theories of learning, arguing that the use of particular discourse strategies reflects certain pedagogical epistemologies (Barnes and Todd, 1995; Wells, 1999; Cazden, 2001; Moyles et al., 2003; Alexander, 2006). It is suggested that the choices teachers make about the kinds of discourse patterns and pedagogical strategies they use in their classrooms are linked to their pedagogical beliefs, and that the most effective teachers are those who can theorise their teaching so as to make confident and professionally informed pedagogic decisions (Askew et al., 1997).

If the classroom discourse is to take a variety of forms and functions as suggested by advocates of dialogic talk, leading to different levels of student participation and engagement, the research reviewed in this chapter suggests teachers will need to pay close attention to their use of question and feedback strategies in order to promote the use of alternative discourse strategies (for example, probing, student questions, uptake questions, teacher statements). Helping teachers to transform classroom talk from the familiar IRF sequence into purposeful and productive dialogue is therefore fundamental to what Tharp and Dalton (2007) see as an alternative 'universalistic' pedagogy. Such an approach to pre and in-service training would emphasise joint teacher–pupil activity and higher-order thinking through a dialogic pedagogy and curriculum which are relevant to the lives and linguistic profile of the communities from which the students come. This research, as Alexander (2006) argues, also suggests the need for dialogic principles to inform professional learning and school improvement.

Research into the professional development of teachers suggests monitoring and self-evaluation will need to become a regular part of in-service training so as to give teachers a degree of ownership of the process of school improvement. Reflection on teachers' intentions and beliefs about their practice is seen as a way of enhancing expert thinking and problem solving in order to bridge the gap between theories and actual classroom practice. Teachers also need opportunities to theorise their teaching so as to make confident and professionally informed decisions about the way they interact with students and that encourage greater participation and higher levels of cognitive engagement.

Studies looking at dimensions of teacher development (e.g. Tharp and Gallimore, 1988; Costa and Garmston, 1994; Joyce and Showers, 1995; Showers and Joyce 1996) suggest that because the instructional behaviours of teachers cannot be influenced until the internal thought processes have been altered, it is essential that teachers have supportive interactions with peers through modelling and feedback if the recitation script is to be changed. Dillon (1994) suggests that coaching and talk-analysis feedback are useful tools for professional development, whereby sympathetic discussion by groups of teachers of data derived from their own classrooms could be an effective starting point. Similarly Moyles et al. (2003) found using video clips of lessons selected by the teacher to be a powerful means of promoting critical reflection on professional practice. Moyles and her colleagues found that their video project, entitled video-stimulated reflective dialogue (VSRD), encouraged teachers to articulate and demonstrate their own understanding of their interactive styles and provided opportunities for monitoring and self-evaluation. In addition to the provision of more powerful professional development programmes, there is the need for more research to provide comprehensive evidence, for both teachers and policy makers, that dialogic styles of teaching encouraging more active student involvement in the guided co-construction of knowledge can produce significant gains in cognitive learning as well as social and emotional benefits.

References

Abd-Kadir, J. and Hardman, F. (2007) 'The discourse of whole-class teaching: a comparative study of Kenyan and Nigerian primary English lessons', *Language and Education* 1 (21): 1–15.

Ackers, J. and Hardman, F. (2000) 'Classroom interaction in Kenyan primary schools', *Compare* 2(31): 245–62.

Alexander, R.J. (2000) *Culture and Pedagogy: International Comparisons in Primary Education.* Oxford: Blackwell.

Alexander, R.J. (2004) *Towards Dialogic Teaching.* York: Dialogos.

Alexander, R.J. (2006) *Towards Dialogic Teaching* (third edition). York: Dialogos.

Askew, M., Brown, M., Rhodes, V., Johnson, D. and Wiliam, D. (1997) *Effective Teachers of Numeracy: Final Report.* London: King's College, University of London.

Barnes, D. and Todd, F. (1977) *Communication and Learning in Small Groups.* Abingdon: Routledge and Kegan Paul.

Barnes, D. and Todd, F. (1995) *Communication and Learning Revisited: Making Meaning Through Talk.* Portsmouth, NH: Heinemann.

Barnes, D., Britton, J. and Rosen, H. (1969) *Language, the Learner and the School.* Harmondsworth: Penguin,

Black, P. and Wiliam, D. (1998) 'Assessment and classroom learning', *Assessment in Education* 1(5): 7–75.

Black, P., Harrison, C., Lee, C., Marshall, B. and Wiliam, D. (2003) *Assessment for Learning: Putting it into Practice.* Maidenhead: Open University Press/McGraw-Hill.

Brown, G. and Wragg, E.C. (1993) *Questioning.* Abingdon: Routledge.

Cazden, C. (2001) *Classroom Discourse: The Language of Teaching and Learning.* Portsmouth, NH: Heinemann.

Costa, A.L. and Garmston, R.J. (1994) *Cognitive Coaching: A Foundation for Renaissance Schools.* Norwood, NJ: Christopher-Gordon.

Dillon, J. (1994) *Using Discussion in Classrooms.* Buckingham: Open University Press.

Edwards, A.D. (1992) '*Teacher talk and pupil competence*', in K. Norman (ed.), *Thinking Voices.* London: Hodder & Stoughton.

Edwards, T., Fitz-Gibbon, C.T., Hardman, F., Haywood, R. and Meagher, N. (1997) *Separate but Equal?: A Levels and GNVQ.* Abingdon: Routledge.

Edwards, D. and Mercer, N. (1987) *Common Knowledge: The Development of Understanding in the Classroom.* Abingdon: Methuen.

Galton, M., Simon, B. and Croll, P. (1980) *Inside the Primary Classroom.* Abingdon: Routledge and Kegan Paul.

Galton, M., Hargreaves, L., Comber, C., Wall, D. and Pell, T. (1999) *Inside the Primary Classroom: 20 Years On.* Abingdon: Routledge.

Hardman, F. (2007) '*The guided co-construction of knowledge*', in N. Hornberger and M. Martin-Jones (eds), *Encyclopedia of Language and Education.* New York: Springer.

Hardman, F., Abd-Kadir, J. and Smith, F. (2008) 'Pedagogical renewal: improving the quality of classroom interaction in Nigerian primary schools', *International Journal of Educational Studies* 28(1): 55–69.

Hardman, F., Abd-Kadir, J., Agg, C., Migwi, J., Ndambuku, J. and Smith, F. (in press) 'Changing pedagogical practice in Kenyan primary schools: the impact of school-based training', *Comparative Education.*

Hardman, F. and Leat, D. (1998) 'Images of post-16 English teaching', *Teaching and Teacher Education* 4(4): 359–68.

Hardman, F. and Mroz, M. (1999) 'Post-16 English teaching: from recitation to discussion', *Educational, Review* 3 (51): 283–93.

Hardman, F. and Williamson, J. (1998) 'The discourse of A level English teaching', *Educational Review,* 1(50): 5–14.

Hardman, F., Smith, F. and Wall, K. (2003) 'Interactive whole-class teaching in the National Literacy Strategy', *Cambridge Journal of Education,* 2(33): 197–215.

Hardman, F., Smith, F. and Wall, K. (2005) 'Teacher–pupil dialogue with pupils with special needs in the National Literacy Strategy', *Educational Review* 3(57): 299–316.

Holquist, M. (1990) *Dialogism: Bakhtin and His World.* Abingdon: Routledge.

Joyce, B. and Showers, B. (1995) *Student Achievement through Staff Development: Fundamentals of School Renewal.* New York: Longman.

Lemke, J.L. (1990) *Talking Science: Language, Learning and Values.* Norwood, NJ: Ablex.

Mercer, N. (1995) *The Guided Construction of Knowledge: Talk Amongst Teachers and Learners.* Clevedon: Multilingual Matters.

Mercer, N. (2000) *Words and Minds: How We Use Language to Think Together.* Abingdon: Routledge.

Moyles, J., Hargreaves, L., Merry, R., Paterson, F. and Esarte-Sarries, V. (2003) *Interactive Teaching in the Primary School.* Maidenhead: Open University Press/McGraw-Hill.

Mroz, M., Smith, F. and Hardman, F. (2000) 'The discourse of the Literacy Hour', *Cambridge Journal of Education* 3(30): 379–90.

Nassaji, H. and Wells, G. (2000) 'What's the use of "Triadic Dialogue"?: an investigation of teacher–student interaction', *Applied Linguistics* 3(21): 376–406.

Nystrand, M., Gamoran, A., Kachur, R. and Prendergast, C. (1997) *Opening Dialogue: Understanding the Dynamics of Language and Learning in the English Classroom.* New York: Teachers College Press.

Nystrand, M., Wu, L.L., Gamoran, A., Zeiser, S. and Long, D.A. (2003) 'Questions in time: investigating the structure and dynamics of unfolding classroom discourse', *Discourse Processes* 2(35): 135–98.

Pontefract, C. and Hardman, F. (2005) 'Classroom discourse in Kenyan primary schools', *Comparative Education* 2(41): 87–106.

Showers, B. and Joyce, B. (1996) 'The evolution of peer coaching', *Educational Leadership* 3(54): 12–16.

Sinclair, J. and Coulthard, M. (1975) *Towards an Analysis of Discourse: The English Used by Teachers and Pupils.* Oxford: Oxford University Press.

Skidmore, D., Perez-Parent, M. and Arnfield, S. (2003) 'Teacher–pupil dialogue in the guided reading session', *Reading: Literacy and Language* 2(37): 47–53.

Smith, F., Hardman, F. and Higgins, S. (2006) 'The impact of interactive whiteboards on teacher–pupil interaction in the National Literacy and Numeracy Strategies', British *Educational Research Journal,* 3(32): 437–51.

Smith, F., Hardman, F. and Higgins, S. (2007) 'Gender inequality in the primary classroom: will interactive whiteboards help?', *Gender and Education,* 4(19): 455–69.

Smith, F., Hardman, F., Wall, K. and Mroz, M. (2004) 'Interactive whole-class teaching in the National Literacy and Numeracy Strategies', *British Educational Research Journal* 3(30): 403–19.

Tharp, R.G. and Dalton, S.S. (2007) 'Orthodoxy, cultural compatibility, and universals in education', *Comparative Education,* 1(43): 53–70.

Tharp, R.G. and Gallimore, R. (1988) *Rousing Minds to Life: Teaching, Learning, and Schooling in Social Context.* Cambridge: Cambridge University Press.

Vygotsky, L.S. (1992) *Thought and Language.* Cambridge, MA: MIT.

Wells, G. (1999) *Dialogic Inquiry: Towards a Sociocultural Practice and Theory of Education.* Cambridge: Cambridge University Press.

Wood, D. (1992) 'Teaching talk', in K. Norman (ed.), *Thinking Voices.* London: Hodder & Stoughton.

Reflections on the Study of Classroom Talk

Courtney Cazden

Summary

This chapter is concerned with how classroom talk links the cognitive, social and cultural aspects of education. The discussion is based on a study of a particular approach to teaching science and literacy in the USA called 'Fostering a community of learners'. Examples are taken from recorded classroom discussions in middle schools using this approach and from interviews with two students some years later, as they reflect on their involvement with it and its impact on their lives. Cazden explains how the approach generated a variety of types of classroom activity, giving the teacher and students opportunities to work together intellectually in different ways, and discusses how these contributed usefully to students' educational experience. She argues that this kind of approach enhances students' control and sense of agency in their education and usefully enables their critical reflection on the process of learning.

For Discussion

1 What were the essential features of the approach used in 'fostering a community of learners'? How do these features relate to your own experiences of education?
2 What activity structures were found to be useful for helping students to 'work on understanding' together?

(Continued)

(Continued)

3   What does Cazden mean by *agency* and *reflection*, and why might they be important for understanding what students gain from education?

4   Can you identify an example of how the approach affected activity on the *social plane*, and of how it influenced individual development.

In 1974, the US National Institute of Education assembled a set of panels to propose an agenda for research on teaching. One panel, which I chaired, was on 'Teaching as a linguistic process in a cultural setting'. To start our planning on some common ground, I asked several people to write papers in advance, including Douglas Barnes. More surprisingly in 1974 than it might be in 2007, Barnes was denied a visa to enter the USA. Despite our protests, he could not attend. But his written words reverberated throughout our panel's deliberations and were prominent in our final report (and in my own later writings; see for example Cazden, 1988/2001). Here they are once more:

> Speech unites the cognitive and the social. The actual (as opposed to the intended) curriculum consists in the meanings enacted or realized by a particular teacher and class. In order to learn, students must use what they already know so as to give meaning to what the teacher presents to them. Speech makes available to reflection the processes by which they relate new knowledge to old. But this possibility depends on the social relationships, the communication system, which the teacher sets up. (National Institute of Education, 1974)

All those who will try to follow these wise words will confront the problem of trying to analyse in detailed ways just *how speech does unite the cognitive and the social*. In the more recent terms of cultural psychologist Barbara Rogoff (1995), how can we best understand relationships among what she calls '*three planes of focus*' separable only for analysis: individual development (the cognitive), social interaction (pre-eminently speech), and the culturally organised activities in which both take place?

It is never easy to argue convincingly about relationships between individual (silent) mental processes and social interactions in any of the activity structures in a typical classroom day. It is easiest in events such as dyadic tutorial sessions (for example Clay and Cazden, 1990), but much harder in the enacted curriculum of a whole class. Here, I will explore relationships among those three planes in one middle-school science and literacy programme that existed in the early 1990s, and then suggest its impact on the subsequent development of some of its graduates who are now in their twenties, as they reflected back on that one-year school experience in interviews with their former teacher in 2004, more than a decade later. My emphasis will be on the complex classroom communication system that is greater than the sum of its separate segments with varied speaking roles in its overall effect.

'Fostering a Community of Learners' (FCL) was designed by psychologists Ann Brown and Joseph Campione in collaboration with two teachers, Marty Rutherford and Doris Ash (Brown et al., 1993; Brown, 1994; Rutherford and Ash, in press) to achieve the dual and reciprocal curriculum goals of science content and academic literacy. It existed in an inner-city public school in Oakland, California, for several years, and became one of the most visible school reform programmes in the USA. The immediate impact of FCL on student learning was documented by the quantitative achievements of its students on standardised literacy tests, and on criterion-referenced tests in both literacy and science that were developed within the programme (Brown and Campione, 1994). (For a detailed analysis of another, more recent, FCL classroom taught by a different teacher, see Engle and Conant, 2002.)

In what follows, I will analyse the 1990s FCL programme according to Rogoff's three planes. Rather than focussing immediately on the middle plane of classroom discourse, I shall begin with the set of culturally organised activities that provide both context and purpose for the speech that enacts them. I will then present two short discourse excerpts from two different activities to show how those purposes affect participation structure and the roles that teachers as well as students take up. In these excerpts, we can hear students 'working on understanding' new scientific concepts (Barnes, this volume) and struggling to express them clearly in writing. Finally, I will quote from the 2004 retrospective interviews of two former FCL students about their memories of their FCL experience and its effect on their longer-term individual development.

I write as a long-time colleague of all four FCL designers, especially psychologist Brown and teacher Rutherford, and as an occasional observer in the FCL classroom and as a co-planner with Rutherford of the retrospective interviews. During 2004–5, I met the two gradu-ates whose interviews are quoted here, and I use their real names here with their full permission.[1]

The culturally organised activities plane

The big curriculum idea was the natural science concept of biological interdependence – first in an introductory unit on the unintended effects of DDT in Borneo (Pomerantz, 1971; a children's book based on a *New York Times* account), and then in a longer multi-month unit on endangered species. Students were organised into research teams. In negotiation with the teacher (T), each team chose from a list of pos-sibilities (panda, alligator, and so on) which animal they would study, then within each animal team, team members negotiated their individual research assignments of one of six features of their team animal (food, habitat, reproduction, communication, defense from enemies, protection from the elements), all of which were essential for survival.

Each team had the responsibility for contributing questions for inclu-sion in a final test that the entire class would take and for a final team report on their research, a significant task that would make their research available to future students and others. They also had the higher-stakes responsibility for teaching the rest of the class what they had learned, both individually and as a team, so that everyone could pass that test on what the class, collectively, now understood.

To engage in what Barnes calls 'working on understanding', the stu-dents had to become socialised into the patterns of participation expected in a set of regularly recurring activity structures: bench-marks, research rotations, jigsaw groups, and cross-talk groups.

Benchmarks were whole-class lecture-discussions led by the teacher. Some were on science concepts – first, to draw out students' initial ideas and later to 'seed' more sophisticated understandings, such as the function of a food chain in how animals become endangered, while others were on academic literacy processes like research skills and building an argument.

Research rotations consisted of several different activities: (a) individual research, reading, note-taking and so on; (b) working at the computer to find new resources, e-mailing classmates or outsiders (such as biology graduate students) for help, or working on their team's report and conferencing about it individually with the teacher; (c) participating, initially under the teacher's guidance, in Reciprocal Teaching (RT) small-group comprehension discussions of texts from books, the Internet, or sections of student reports.

Developed a decade before FCL (Palincsar, 1984), Reciprocal Teaching was designed as an external interactional support, or scaffold, for practising the internal cognitive activities that expert readers perform. It provides practice in four comprehension strategies: questioning the main points; clarifying vocabulary, concepts and inferences; summarising the main points in a paragraph or section; and where appropriate predicting what event or information may follow. Initially modelled by the teacher, this discussion format becomes less formalised as it is appropriated by the students through repeated use, first with the teacher and then without her.

Jigsaw groups occurred periodically, as research teams became more knowledgeable about their subtopics and a student from each team met in an ad hoc Jigsaw group (Aronson, 1997) with a member of each of the other teams and taught them (typically for as long as 30 minutes) the results of their research, sometimes by 'RTing' (as the students called it) a relevant text or a section of their team's report. (The importance of these small groups in the overall FCL design is another connection to Barnes's work.)

Cross-talk occurred when the students themselves realised that Jigsaw teaching required them to know all about their team's animal, not just their individual feature, and they suggested arranging a time when they could bring their research to the whole class and exchange thinking while their work was still in progress. They named this activity 'cross-talk'. In a panel presentation at the April 2006 (San Francisco) meeting of the American Educational Research Association, Rutherford and former FCL students agreed that cross-talk was an example of how students contributed to the overall programme design.

What is missing from this skeletal description of the different forms of social organisation that constituted this classroom as a learning system is the excitement that the students came to feel about their

FCL experience. One student, Jonathan Davis, talked about this in his (2004) interview:

> The DDT project, when it was first presented to us, I thought I didn't even know where Borneo is. I could have cared less about mosquitoes and malaria and DDT. As the project went on, you embraced it. It wasn't just the topic; it was an interesting topic, but for an 11-year-old boy, it wasn't your first choice to talk about DDT and some disease you never heard of in a country you never heard of … .

> But it was kind of like how we did the structure of the class that made the stuff interesting because it made you feel like an adult. When you were young, everybody wants to feel like an adult. The class was very mature and adult … It kind of pushed you to do your work … to do more work than you would have done if it were just the normal sixth grade experience. I think for the most part *the class helped the content more than the content helped the class*. (emphasis added)

There's a powerful hypothesis for pedagogy here in Jonathan's final comment that 'the class helped the content more than the content helped the class'. The 'relevance' of the curriculum for students is so often judged in terms of literal, obvious connections between curriculum topics and students' out-of-school lives and interests as they enter the classroom. Jonathan remembers how his initially low interest developed through his participation in 'the class'. In other words, he can be heard saying that he got 'caught up' by, and engaged with, social relationships in the FCL classroom before, and as the medium through which, he became engaged with the intellectual curriculum content. What Jonathan names simply as 'the class', visiting psychologist Jerome Bruner (1996) calls the 'culture' that teacher and students 'construct, negotiate, and institutionalise' together.

Elsewhere in his interview, Jonathan talks about specific memorable features of 'the class', including 'the group process thing', 'the structure of the class', 'the open communication with the teachers', 'a lot of feedback, give and take', 'when you have to present your work … [and] the questions that the students or teachers would ask you'. Then in responding to Rutherford's question about possible relevance to his current work as a teacher, Jonathan declares, 'FCL showed to me, or to whoever was in the class, or who witnessed it, what kids are capable of doing.'

The interpersonal plane: Classroom discourse

Two brief segments of classroom discourse (both quoted in their entirety from Rutherford and Ash, in press) will show two of the diverse participation structures in the above set of interlocked activities that together constitute the 'interpersonal plane' in the FCL programme. In the first excerpt from a cross-talk group, we can hear students 'working on understanding' scientific concepts. In the second, different students are working equally hard on expressing in writing what they have learned so that others can use their text as a research resource.

Cross-talk discussion

In this excerpt, 'The students … were working to build a shared understanding of the notion of the biological advantages and disadvantages of certain animal survival adaptations' (Rutherford and Ash, in press). Here, the discussion topic becomes how, or whether, female size affects the survival feature of reproduction.

LaSaundra: This [size] is an advantage because if she [peregrine falcon] is bigger, therefore she can produce more babies, because she has enough womb to make a lot more babies than if she was smaller than the male.

T: Stop right there guys. What LaSaundra said is what I came to, but I don't know if I'm right. Let's go back to the original words: sexual dimorphism, survival and success … All things being equal, it's OK for the female to be bigger and if she is bigger, can't she lay more eggs? If she lays more eggs, can't she have more big babies? If she has more babies, isn't she going to survive and be more successful?

Michael: She's not going to have more babies because humans are bigger than peregrines, and they only have one baby, sometimes twins. Nwaoha?

Nwaoha: It doesn't matter, Michael. Human is different from a bird. Different kinds of birds lay more eggs than each other. Snakes aren't birds, and they lay more eggs than birds.

Joe: Humans have … humans have less babies. Florencia?

Florencia: Michael, you're wrong because, like what Nwaoha said, we don't look like birds … We don't have feathers … We are different from peregrine falcons, so I don't understand why you are comparing.

Hanadora: It depends on the size of the baby … Human babies are bigger than baby birds.

Note first the teacher's role. She takes the floor firmly, but not in the prototypical teacher's role of evaluating LaSaundra's statement, or even giving feedback on her idea that size is inherently an adaptive advantage. Instead, as an observer can only understand after the fact, as the discussion continues T's intervention serves to expand the questions that the student's statement raises and holds the place for further group consideration of them. The fact that she accomplishes this by initially aligning herself with LaSaundra additionally serves to prevent either LaSaundra herself or anyone else from inferring any critical evaluation.

Substantively, the five other students then take up T's challenge to think harder about the issues raised by LaSaundra's draft – namely, the possible survival value of a larger female in one species, the peregrine falcon. One source of factual background knowledge is what they all know experientially about another species, humans. Florencia then raises the significant conceptual issue of when cross-species comparison (and by implication all background knowledge) is, or is not, relevant.

Structurally, the students talk with and to each other, not back to T. They respond to Michael by name, designate by name ('Nwaoha', 'Florencia') who is to be the next speaker, and always maintain a respectful tone, especially through supporting their comments and criticism ('Michael, you're wrong …') with reasons that leave openings ('So I don't under-stand …') for the student criticised to come back with further thoughts. (See Michaels et al. (2007) for an extensive discussion, with examples, of academically productive discourse in science classrooms.)

Reciprocal teaching discussion

'FCL classrooms were intentionally organized to foster the acquisi-tion of the kind of language that led learning and expressing new, complex ideas' (Rutherford and Ash, in press). The following tran-script illustrates this point. At the beginning of this exchange Tiffany is presenting a section of her group's paper that she had written. Then she invites RT-type discussion.

Tiffany: (Reading from her paper) 'Orangutan reproduction. After mating the male and female orangutan usually stay together for the whole length of pregnancy. Eight and a half-months after mating, the female orangutan will give birth to a baby. When the baby orang-utan is born it is very weak and helpless, but it is still able to hold onto its mother after birth. The young orangutan will depend on its mother for food, warmth, and transportation for a long period of time. The mother and baby orangutan will usually stay together for six or seven years because it takes that long for the offspring to be able to be on its own. Even at the age of four, the baby orangutan still needs to be with its mother. If you think about it, that is a long time especially when you are comparing [it] to other animals. Most animals, such as baby whales, stay with its mother until it is between the ages of two and six months old.' Summaries? Questions? Clarifications?

Hana: I can summarise. I think this talks about how the baby orangutan depends on its mother and how they can't live without the mother.

Nicole: I had a question on page seven where it says that the orangutan is becoming an endangered species. I thought it already was. It's becoming one?

Tiffany: When I said that it is becoming an endangered species I meant that it is becoming more endangered than it has been before. It probably was endangered before, but to me they are real close to extinction because there are so few in the world. But that's a really good question that you pointed out, and others might point that out too so now that you told me about this I should state it more clearly.

Nicole: The orangutan was real similar in some ways to the panda. It's like if it was taken away from its mother and put in a zoo, it couldn't survive. It's like the same thing, but since it's so much more intelligent than the panda, I think that's why it stays with its mother for a longer time because with the panda, it only stays for a short amount of time. I just wanted to say to Marty (T) after reading about different kinds of reproduction … I realised that I'm kind of familiar with that in other animals. It's like I notice how much I have to fix in my report' cause I think about so much about what it has to do with pandas and I know that I didn't include it.

As the writer whose text is to be discussed, Tiffany sets out her initial request for three important comprehension strategies: summarising and/or questioning main ideas, and clarifying specific points. After those responses, Nicole then suggests an interesting, if seemingly more tangential, hypothesis about the relationship between time spent with a mother in a species and that species' 'intelligence', using for her comparative species not the shared experiential knowledge of humans (as in the first excerpt above), but her individual research knowledge about pandas. She then makes a side comment directly to T (a hitherto silent presence in the group) about her awareness of how she has to expand her own panda report.

While parts of Tiffany's paper may seem at first glance, and without access to prior drafts, to be unproductively close to what may have been her textual resources, the teacher realised that the amount of detail also reflected Tiffany's intense interest in her chosen feature of reproduction, and in variations in how long mothers and their babies stay together (Rutherford, personal communication, August, 2007).

The plane of individual development: two students' 2004 reflections

The FCL students were overwhelmingly children of colour. One article about the programme gives statistics for 'one representative sixth-grade class': 60 per cent African American, 15 per cent Asian, 12 per cent Caucasian, 6 per cent Pacific Islanders, 7 per cent other, with almost half of their families receiving free or reduced-cost lunch (Brown et al., 1993: 195.) The five students whom Rutherford was able to find, and who were willing to participate in the 2004 interviews, were African American or Pacific Islander: three young women and two young men. The two whose interviews I will quote here are Jonathan Davis (already quoted above about his evolving engagement) and Florencia Tuaumu. Jonathan Davis [African American] is working as a journalist and teaching coach while he finishes his BA and gets his teaching credential, and Florencia Tuaumu [Samoan American] has finished a pre-med course and is now attending medical school.

In order to categorise excerpts from Jonathan's and Felicia's lengthy individual interviews to present as evidence for the impact of their FCL experience on their individual development, I have adopted two of the underlying design features identified by Jerome Bruner (1996) after his visit to the FCL classroom – *agency* and *reflection*.

Agency
By 'agency', Bruner refers to 'taking control of your own mental activity'. Alternatively, Australian David Hogan, director of the Centre for Research on Pedagogy and Practice in Singapore, defines agency as 'voluntary, intentional social action by actors to secure specific goals or objectives in particular social contexts' (Discussion Paper v.21, 2005; personal communication, February, 2007).

Florencia speaks about what entering FCL meant to her after several years in a more typical inner-city school:

> I came from a school that was in threat of being closed down due to increased violence, and a curriculum that was practically deadening and very non-effective to say the least ...
>
> When I take my mind back to the first day that I *sat* in that classroom and saw the excitement ... I couldn't help but feel excited myself; it was as if a spark of intellectual hope and potential had been ignited. I don't know whether that was intended but it was truly felt ... Sitting there hearing what we were about to do was like, at least for me, a starved child being shown a meal fit for a king. My mind was the hungry child and I could feel myself grown eager in the hopes that I could be filling my *mind* to its fullest potential. It was almost like a mind homecoming of sorts. It was something we had *always* been able to do but never actually had the chance, and now, the possibilities were seemingly endless.
>
> I never had that opportunity before ... Most teachers I had already interacted with didn't care about me or what I had to say let alone *think* ... They only cared if you listened – even if they were talking about nothing. The [FCL] project made me feel like the opportunities were limitless ...
>
> We were given a free hand to read, write, learn, teach and most of all – grow. (emphasis in original)

Actively feeling a 'spark of intellectual hope and potential', a 'mind homecoming', where teachers cared about what she thought and where 'opportunities were limitless' – in contrast to classrooms where teachers only cared if students 'listened, even if they were talking about nothing' – these are signs of a dramatic shift in Florencia's sense of agency.

Jonathan's sense of agency is expressed in the ways he concretises aspects of the 'freedoms' that were available. To him, the significant choices were not of topics, as in what animal or what adaptive feature one could research, but of the cognitively more significant approach or stance one could take:

> By freedom – yes, we had our assignments, and roles, and some of the stuff that was supposed to be addressed in the paper was mandatory. But you could take different angles ... There wasn't a right answer, and it was one of the first times in school where there wasn't, like, 'Here is the question and it is one right answer.' There were plenty of right answers. So you had the freedom to approach the topic or approach the question however you wanted, as long as you came away making some kind of sense or some kind of logic and reason.

Another aspect of his sense of 'freedom' came from the teacher's trust in the students that made possible the freedom of physical movement that in turn enabled collaboration during non-official group times of the day:

> Like I didn't have to raise my hand to go to one of my team mate's desk to ask them about, you know, what do you think about crocodiles and reproduction, or do you have any notes about DDT and Borneo? ... I guess it was the trust thing, and once we gained the trust it was easy going from there. But it was like the trust was always there. Like from the first day, like this is how it is going to be. And that's how it was.

Reflection

Bruner defines reflection as 'making sense, going "meta", turning around on what one has learned ... , even thinking about one's thinking' (1996: 88). Under various names (meta-cognitive awareness, self-monitoring, and so on) reflection has become a prominent objective of strategic teaching for 'learning how to learn'. As with 'agency', we can infer 'reflection' from what our two students say in their more experiential language. Florencia states:

> I had gotten into the habit at one time of just taking the exact thing out of the book, and [the teacher] would ask me, 'OK, but how would *you* say it?'... It was one thing for me to revise and reform an idea, but at the same time that idea would manifest itself differently in the paper itself ... I have to put that concept into play with the *whole* question being asked. If the topic was sea otters, then I had to take my idea back and fit it into the big picture concerning *sea otters* and so forth. Putting it into motion was different than *knowing* it itself. (emphasis in original)

As Jonathan's description of the evolution of his engagement with FCL suggested a powerful hypothesis for pedagogy, so too does Florencia's final comment: 'putting that concept [what she knew from her own individual research] into play with the *whole* question being asked ... putting it into motion was different from *knowing* it itself'. In FCL's enacted curriculum, putting one's individually generated ideas into 'play' and 'motion' is required by the set of collaborative activities, especially the jigsaw model of teaching.

Jonathan expressed the same idea is his interview:

> When you have to explain your positions, thoughts, and beliefs more thoroughly, it helps to have an open mind. Because when you delve deeper into your reasoning or logic, you usually see similarities between your view and different opposing views.

Collaborative activities are advocated today for various reasons: to motivate engagement, to stimulate civic responsibility, to develop discourse skills of explaining and group problem solving as well as listening closely to others. We may not normally think about their possible additional effect on more internal cognition: only when you have to explain an idea to someone else successfully do you realise just what you do and do not understand.

Early in *The Culture of Education*, Bruner says that he will 'constantly be enquiring about the interaction between the powers of individual minds and the means by which the culture aids or thwarts their realization' (1996: 13). Later, he expresses this theme more concretely: 'In the Oakland project, Ann Brown has joined agency and collaboration together in the design of classroom culture ... They [agency and collaboration] need to be treated together, else learning is made to seem either too solo or not solo enough' (1996: 93, 92).

This way of conceiving the relationship between individual learning and development and the recurring activities in a specific educational culture inevitably raises the question of the impact of FCL beyond the one fifth or sixth grade year that students were at in that class. In answer to Rutherford's final question about any such impact, Florencia spoke eloquently about how what she took from FCL sustained her during her subsequent, barren school years:

> There was a time in *high school* where I hit a slump and I had a moment of self-evaluation as to why I felt that way. I realised learning wasn't fun anymore for me; I had to sit down and remember when it was. The FCL period was that for me. That experience gave me something to look back on to remember and *hold* on to. I told my mother that FCL introduced me to that state of mind that *loved* to learn. That passion and thirst for learning was one of the many things that is still with me today ... my whole thought process was shaped from that one significant period in my life. They were encouraging us. They wanted us to succeed. They spoke as if we were destined to succeed. People believed in you every step of the way, leading us to believe that the knowledge was ours to possess. Being able to have that 'power' was what made all the difference. When I would feel myself getting mentally drained or exhausted I would remember the FCL project – the prospect and hopes I had for myself.

> To think back on FCL was a boost of learning adrenaline ... I was David and ignorance was Goliath and I knocked it stone cold.

Jonathan and Florencia's articulateness in their interviews raises a second question, for research as well as education, about how representative of FCL these two students can be considered. They were, after all, selected for this chapter from the five students interviewed, and these five were simply the only ones Rutherford could contact after more than a decade.

My argument for using their words as evidence about the FCL programme itself rests on the unusual degree of cohesion and coherence built into the design of the FCL classroom through the psychologist/teacher collaboration during its development. Such cohesion and coherence comes from the interlocking structures of obligatory collaborative work and collective responsibility. The amount of individual variability in engagement and uptake so characteristic of most classroom environments should, for that reason, be reduced.

Conclusion

At a Singapore conference on 'Redesigning Pedagogy', Gunter Kress began by asserting, 'Among the many changes that have overtaken education, one of the most profound is the shift from the focus on teaching to a focus on learning' (2007: 19).

FCL is one example of a classroom organised for learning. My purpose in describing its organisational details is not to advocate the replication of any or all of them. Consider just one structure central to FCL's overall design – jigsawing. US math educator Alan Schoenfeld has analysed the problems in trying to enact it across the curriculum in his commentary on reports of attempts to re-enact FCL in four curriculum subjects: social studies, science (biology), English language arts, and mathematics:

> All four papers testify to its [jigsawing's] difficulty for one of two reasons: (a) not all big ideas lend themselves easily to the process of decomposing and recombining that lies at the heart of the jigsaw method, and (b) some of the 'natural' methods of constructing jigsaws may demand competencies that extend far beyond that of most teachers (or designers or researchers) …

> As has been seen, jigsawing turns out to be easy in some cases, near impossible in others: to require it – even though it gives a distinct signature to FCL lessons – is to overconstrain instructional design. Rather the goal should be to operate in a spirit consistent with the goals and principles that underlie jigsawing … Some topics or units in almost any intellectual domain will be suitable for jigsawing and many will not. (Shoenfeld, 2004: 245)

Suggestions for generalisability come not from specific structures but from FCL's design features. Different sets of such features have been suggested. As discussed above, Bruner (1996) lists four: agency, collaboration, reflection, and culture. Without citing Bruner, Schoenfeld gives a similar list: 'The four FCL principles of learning are activity, reflection, collaboration, and community' (2004: 238). Ann Brown (1994), in explaining the genesis of FCL, gives seven. And collaborating teacher Rutherford added two of her own: 'learning stuff that matters' and teachers acting on the 'belief that kids are smart' (personal communication in response to an earlier version of this chapter, August 2005).

References

Aronson, E. (1997) *The Jigsaw Classroom: Building Cooperation in the Classroom* (second ed). New York: Longman.

Brown, A.L. (1994) 'The advancement of learning', *Educational Researcher*, 23 (8): 4–12.

Brown, A.L. and Campione, J.C. (1994) 'Guided discovery in a community of learners', in K. McGilly (ed.), *Classroom Lessons: Integrating Cognitive Theory and Classroom Practice*. Cambridge, MA: MIT Press.

Brown, A.L., Ash, D., Rutherford, M. et al. (1993) 'Distributed expertise in the classroom', in G. Salomon (ed.), *Distributed Cognitions*. New York: Cambridge University Press.

Bruner, J. (1996) *The Culture of Education*. Cambridge, MA: Harvard University Press.

Cazden, C.B. (1998/2001). *Classroom Discourse: The Language of Teaching and Learning (2nd ed.)*. Portsmouth, MA: Heinemann.

Clay, M. and Cazden, C.B. (1990) 'A Vygotskian interpretation of Reading Recovery', in L.C. Moll (ed.), *Vygotsky and Education: Instructional Implications and Applications of Sociohistorical Psychology*. New York: Cambridge University Press. pp. 206–22.

Engle, R.A. and Conant, F.R. (2002) 'Guiding principles for fostering productive disciplinary engagement: explaining an emergent argument in a community of learners' classroom', *Cognition and Instruction*, 20 (4): 399–483.

Kress, G. (2007) 'Thinking about meaning and learning in a world of instability and multiplicity', *Pegagogies: An International Journal*, 2 (1): 19–34.

Michaels, S., Shouse, A. and Schweingruber, H. (2007) *Ready, Set, Science: Putting Research to Work in the K-8 Science Classroom*. Washington, DC: National Academy Press.

Palincsar, A.S. (1984) 'The role of dialogue in scaffolded instruction', *Educational Psychologist*, 21: 73–98.

Pomerantz, C. (1971) *The Day They Parachuted Cats on Borneo: A Drama of Ecology*. Reading, MA: Addison Wesley.

Rogoff, B. (1995) 'Sociocultural activity on three planes: participatory appropria-
tion, guided participation, and apprenticeship', in J.V. Wertsch, P. Del Rio and
A. Alvarez (eds), *Sociocultural Studies of Mind*. New York: Cambridge University
Press. pp. 139–64.

Rutherford, M. and Ash, D. (in press). 'The legacy of Ann Brown: Still learning
after all these years'. In J.C. Compione, K. Metz and A.S. Palincsar (eds.)
*Children's Learning in the Laboratory and in the Classroom: Esays in Honor of Ann
Brown*. Mahwah, NJ: Erlbaum.

Schoenfeld, A.H. (2004) 'Multiple learning communities: students, teachers,
instructional designers, and researchers', *Journal of Curriculum Studies* , 36 (2):
237–55.

Note

1   I am indebted to FCL teacher Marty Rutherford for continuing conversations over the
years about all the issues raised in this paper. Support for the 2004 interview project
is gratefully acknowledged from the Spencer Foundation Senior Scholar grant to
Courtney Cazden.

10

Exploratory Talk and Dialogic Inquiry

Gordon Wells and Tamara Ball

 Summary

In this chapter, Wells and Ball explain how an inquiry approach to teaching and learning can help generate more productive dialogue and exploratory talk in the classroom. The chapter is based on their analysis of whole-class discussions and group activity in primary/ elementary schools in the USA on which this approach was implemented and evaluated, and also draws on the reflections of a group of teachers who were actively involved in the research. They give special consideration to the role of the teacher in making inquiry and associated discussion meaningful and interesting for pupils. They conclude with a summary of conditions which their research indicates can help classroom talk become most productive as pupils pursue their curriculum-related inquiries.

For Discussion

1 What are the main requirements for making a classroom a 'community of inquiry'?
2 What were the observable effects on discourse of creating a community of inquiry?
3 How can teachers use this approach to link talk with texts in a productive way?

(Continued)

(Continued)
4 Can you outline an activity for using this approach in the schools with which you are familiar?
5 What implications does the research Wells and Ball describe have for understanding the role of the teacher, and for teacher-training?

In talk and writing about education, 'learning', 'meaning' and 'understanding' are provocatively ambivalent words. Official documents, such as curriculum standards and guidelines, frequently use them to refer to *products* and *outcomes* that can be measured as evidence of the effectiveness (or ineffectiveness) of individual lessons or whole courses of study. However, their linguistic '-ing' form points to an alternative interpretation, that is to say, the active mental *processing* through which meanings are created and learning occurs. One of Douglas Barnes's greatest contributions to the field of education has been to insist that we need to give much greater attention to these *processes* if we are to ensure that the 'products' are of lasting value. Note the verb forms (italicised) in the first sentence of the following extract from his chapter in this volume.

> Most of our important *learning*, in school or out, is a matter of *constructing* models of the world, *finding* how far they work by using them, and then *reshaping* them in the light of what happens. Each new model or scheme potentially changes how we experience some aspect of the world, and therefore how we act on it.

In these words, he makes very clear that the purpose of schooling is not to acquire large quantities of (inert) knowledge – which Freire (1970) has referred to as the 'banking' model of education – but rather to increase continually one's understanding in order to act effectively and responsibly when faced with challenging situations. Furthermore, like Dewey (1938) he believes that, for students to develop this lifelong disposition, the learning activities in which they engage in school should involve 'exploratory talk' and be focussed on 'working on understanding'.

Our aim in this chapter is to extend the discussion of the value of 'exploratory talk' in learning for understanding by focussing on the conditions that foster and support this kind of interaction and on how those conditions can be created, particularly in whole-class discussion.

Developing dialogic through inquiry

Given the long-term dominance of information transmission in the history of schooling (Cole, 1996), it is not surprising that, despite repeated calls for a more dialogic form of interaction, transmission remains the default option in most classrooms. On the one hand, teachers have themselves been socialised to accept the assumed necessity for this genre of classroom talk through their own experiences as students (even in their professional preparation, in many cases), and on the other hand, students also very quickly discover that success depends on learning to perform according to the conventions of this genre. Furthermore, this 'recitation script' (Tharp and Gallimore, 1988), with its basic structure of teacher or text-book exposition followed by sequences of I–R–E exchanges (teacher initation – student response – teacher evaluation), seems to be ideally suited to the current emphasis on improving test scores as the evidence of successful teaching and learning. As a result, students will seek agreement and alignment with their superiors rather than questioning or proposing alternatives, being aware that if they can discover and provide the response envisaged by their superior they are more likely to succeed. However, these 'positional' relationships do not create a classroom ethos that is conducive to dialogue and exploratory talk.

In recent years, considerable research effort has been devoted to ways of overcoming the preponderance of transmission, and with some positive effects. Teachers allowing increased 'wait time' after asking a question, and before asking it again or providing the answer themselves, has been found to increase both student participation and the quality of their answers. Even more important is the recognition that asking questions to which there is not just one 'known answer' is more likely to elicit multiple alternative answers and perhaps to provoke discussion (Cazden, 1988). In addition, giving students time to prepare their thoughts about an issue or question – either through individual writing or in small groups – prior to a whole-class discussion greatly increases the diversity of contributions (Brown et al., 1993).

Nevertheless, despite the evidence of the value of these teaching strategies, few teachers are likely to persist with them if they attempt to adopt them as piecemeal changes to their 'normal' way of conducting discussion. For, as long as teachers retain a vision of teaching as ensuring that students 'learn' and remember the material predefined by the curricular guidelines, they are likely to abandon the new strategies as soon as the pressure to 'cover' the prescribed content becomes too severe. To bring about a lasting change a different vision of teaching is required, one that goes beyond a concern with the use of appropriate discourse moves to a recognition of the centrality of dialogue as a means of developing both group and individual understanding, coupled with the recognition that productive dialogue does not proceed independent of the activity and activity goals it mediates.

What we are suggesting, therefore, is that it is when students are directly involved and have a 'sense of agency' in the ongoing activity that they are most interested and motivated to engage in dialogue, because it is then that they have something they want to contribute. Research has shown that, in the preschool years, most of children's learning occurs as an integral part of engaging in activities in which they *do* have, or are developing, an interest (Wells, 1986; Nelson, 2007) and the same continues to be true of their later learning outside of school. The question, then, is how to create similar conditions in the classroom while still meeting the externally imposed 'standards'.

In trying to find an answer to this question, we have been much influenced by two key figures: Vygotsky and Dewey. Vygotsky (1987), and the cultural–historical activity theory that he initiated, emphasise the central role of dialogue in taking over and making one's own the knowledge, skills and practices that enable one to participate productively in the activities of one's community and of the wider society; he also explained how, by receiving assistance in thinking together with others, one transforms one's ability to engage autonomously in thinking, planning and reflecting on action in the dialogue of 'inner speech'. From Dewey, we learned the motivational importance of inquiry. Writing about the kind of education that he had pioneered in his experimental school in Chicago, Dewey (1938) argued that children's learning should occur as an integral aspect of inquiry, arising from significant and often problematic features of their experience and environment, and should have as its intended outcome a growth in their understanding – by which he meant not simply factual knowledge, but knowledge growing out of, and oriented to, socially relevant and productive action.

Furthermore, like Vygotsky, Dewey believed that one of the most important functions of inquiry was to generate occasions for purposeful dialogue. When students pursue investigations, he argued, they develop ideas and acquire information that they want to share and debate; at the same time, the problems they encounter call for the joint consideration of alternative possible solutions. In these circumstances, students have a reason to learn the skills necessary for engaging in productive dialogue and, over time, they also develop the disposition to approach problem solving of all kinds in this way, which will be of value both to them in the future and to the larger society of which they are becoming members.

In Dewey's conception of the ideal classroom, the topics for inquiry were to be generated by individual students, in relation to which the teacher's role was to act as facilitator rather than as instructor. Vygotsky, on the other hand, placed much greater emphasis on collaborative group investigation. This was in part because he saw the social group, in this case the classroom community, as the source from which the individual appropriated the meaning making practices that are the foundation of higher mental functions. But equally important was the much more active role he assigned to the teacher in selecting the topics for students' inquiries and in providing direction and guidance as they engaged in the problem solving to which these inquiries were intended to give rise (Glassman, 2001). For it was in such situations that the teacher was able to work most effectively with students in their 'zones of proximal development' (Vygotsky, 1987).

In the early 1990s, a number of educational researchers in North America were experimenting with what might be seen as a combination of the ideas of Vygotsky and Dewey, reinterpreted in relation to contemporary schools. This was also the point of departure for the project started by the first author of this chapter at this time, but with one significant difference. If teachers were to adopt an 'inquiry orientation to the curriculum', we argued, they also needed to be inquirers in their own classrooms, both investigating the effectiveness of different ways of creating an ethos of inquiry and providing a model of 'the inquiring learner' for their students. So we decided to invite a number of teachers who had expressed an interest in teacher research to form a group to carry out collaborative action research with us in the Developing Inquiring Communities in Education Project (DICEP). However, we soon realised that, rather than focussing directly on the discourse of inquiry, what was needed was a more explicit focus on the conditions that could give rise to inquiry (Wells, 1999).

With this aim, each member designed and carried out investigations in which they focussed on the effectiveness of a variety of ways in which they were trying to create a community of inquiry in their classrooms. These included introducing classroom meetings, incorporating more practical investigatory work and role play, and organising explicit opportunities for student 'performances of understanding'. At their invitation, lessons were video recorded and transcribed and these recordings often provided data for joint discussion in our monthly meetings. Periodically, the group agreed to adopt a common theme, such as the potential roles of writing in supporting inquiry. The final theme in the period during which the group was externally funded was that of including students as 'coinvestigators'.[1] From early on in its history, many members of the group also began to organise joint presentations at conferences and to write articles to disseminate what they were learning through their collaborative research (see for example, Wells, 2001). In the following section we describe some of the changes that took place over the course of the DICEP project.

The discursive effects of creating communities of inquiry

In all, we video recorded 45 episodes of teacher/whole-class discussion in grades one through eight over a seven-year period. We also collected about the same number of episodes of small-group discussion, but these were not included in the quantitative analyses. The first analysis we carried out was based on categorising the episodes according to the overall function of each episode in relation to the curriculum unit in which it occurred. Here what we found was that the interaction became more dialogic when the class was engaged in such activities as planning, interpreting, or reviewing student inquiries. By contrast, episodes of teacher-led instruction, classroom management, and checking on what had been learned tended to be characterised by shorter sequences of talk on a particular issue and a higher proportion of evaluative responses to student contributions (Nassaji and Wells, 2000).

The second analysis divided the recorded episodes according to when they occurred in each teacher's participation in the project. By comparing 'early' with 'late' episodes, we found a number of significant changes, which can be summarised as follows:

- Over the duration of the seven-year project, there was a sustained and successful attempt to adopt an inquiry orientation to the curriculum and this, in turn, led to a more negotiatory and dialogic style of interaction.

- More specifically, comparing late with early episodes, there was a decrease in the proportion of sequences initiated by a teacher question and, correlatively, a significant increase in student initiation of sequences.

- When the teacher did initiate with a question s/he was more likely to request information that opened up discussion rather than calling for known information.

- Following student answers, there was a significant increase in the frequency with which teachers provided high-level evaluation, either by taking up and developing the student's contribution or by inviting the same or a different student to do so. There was also a significant increase in the frequency with which the teachers did not take up the option of giving follow up, thereby allowing the discourse to proceed in a more dialogic style.

On the basis of these results, we concluded that an inquiry orientation to the curriculum does indeed make dialogic interaction involving exploratory talk more likely to occur. We also concluded that 'the single most important action a teacher can take to shift the interaction from monologic to dialogic is to ask questions to which there are multiple possible answers and then to encourage the students who wish to answer to respond to, and build upon, each other's contributions' (Wells and Mejía Arauz, 2006).

Through the teachers' eyes

Another way of providing evidence of the changes summarised above is by looking at what the teachers wrote about their own inquiries and how they saw the effect of the changes that they were making in their teaching. For example, two teachers decided to institute regular classroom meetings in order to give their students an opportunity to discuss what was happening in their classrooms and how they thought they could make them function better as communities. In each case, this led to students carrying over the discursive practices these meetings involved to their participation in discussions about curricular topics.

Greta Davis systematically investigated this carry-over by comparing the discussion in class meetings with the discussions that followed her serial reading aloud of a novel to her third grade class. As well as recording the discussions, she also interviewed the children to discover their perspectives on what they had been doing. Here is her commentary on what she learned.

> As in the class meetings, students commented on the value of opportunities to construct knowledge together by listening to each other's ideas. Their comments also demonstrated an awareness of the impact of collaboration on their own thinking. The students were asked what value they saw in novel discussions compared to their previous experiences involving the writing of story summaries and the answering of questions. Many felt more was learned from novel discussions because greater emphasis was placed on their ideas. ... As teachers, we are sometimes quick to judge that a student does not understand when they cannot answer our questions. Turning the discussion over to the students is a means of opening new doors to understanding for all members of the community. (Davis, 2001)

Karen Hume took a different route. In a class she was taking at the university, she read about the work of Scardamalia and Bereiter (1994) in developing what they called 'collaborative knowledge building' through the use of networked computers (CSILE). This technology enabled students to communicate their ideas about investigations they were carrying out by typing and saving them for other students to critique or develop on the central computer database. Karen was very impressed by the discussions that resulted and decided to introduce the practice of collaborative knowledge building into her combined grade 6 and 7 class. However, not having enough computers to reproduce the same format, she decided to use a large bulletin board instead. When questions arose in the course of their investigations, students posted them on the 'Knowledge Wall' and, as in CSILE, other students continued the dialogue by posting comments or questions below the opening question.

In one particular unit, her students were studying the causes and consequences of the Black Death in medieval Europe and, in the materials they were reading, some students were intrigued by references to, and illustrations of, the protective clothing worn by doctors. One student posted a question on the Knowledge Wall and, as the following written notes show, the students used conjecture, evidence from published material, and reasoning to attempt to construct a satisfying answer to their question.

Question: Why did an odd bird figure in a cloak protect doctors?

(referring to an image from a history book showing a doctor clad in leather and wearing a beak mask that makes him look like a bird)

Ian: I don't have a total answer for this, but the paragraph underneath the picture says that the bird mask is to filter out the polluted air, and the wand is to heal patients. Don't ask me why he/she wears a leather cloak.

Eren: If what this guy is wearing is a mask, it might have actually helped him stay healthy.

Alec: This is good, Ian, but why a bird/man/penguin?

Justin: At the end of the caption of the bird figure, in quotes, it claims, 'doctors hoped to avoid the contagion by looking more like a crow than a man'.

          Can anybody try to clarify the quote?

Alec: Why a crow?

Suzanne: People probably wanted to be birds because they saw that the birds weren't dying. This is because birds don't get fleas and fleas caused the Black Death.

Matt: It was not the bird figure protecting the doctors like a god, but it is a form of disease proof clothing. The beak is an early form of gas mask, the cloak of heavy leather. The wand is for soothing the patients. The doctor is covered from head to toe, therefore keeping out the disease.

Ray: Theoretically, the birdlike cloak thing might prevent the fleas from getting to the doctors skin, thus giving the individual the plague. The cloak was basically a shield.

Suzanne: This could and probably is true, but I doubt the people of the time knew that.

Jon: I think it is a witch doctor because of what he is wearing.

Justin: It is just a doctor dressed in leather wearing an early edition of a gas mask. More like a doctor wearing a shield from the fleas.

Suzanne: But, Justin, the doctor didn't KNOW that fleas cause the disease, therefore he couldn't have been wearing it for protection. That's why I agree with Jon that yes, the doctor probably is a witch doctor.

          The bird suit only had a spiritual meaning.

Justin: I didn't say that he/she knew. I mean that the doctor was using the leather as a shield.

While this written dialogue is not a whole-class discussion as such, it grew out of the oral discussions that were a regular part of Karen's way of teaching and allowed the students to continue the discussion in a more sustained manner than is possible in the face-to-face mode. However, there was also a great deal of oral discussion as students gathered at the Knowledge Wall to read and discuss the latest postings and to formulate their responses. As is clear from the talk above, what motivated and sustained this collaborative investigation was the sense that the students had of tackling a question that was of real, shared interest to them. Commenting on this, Karen Hume wrote:

> This speaks to the importance of a round of whole-class and small group activity *before* attempting to work with student questions. The common base that we had built [in this way] not only provided us with a number of shared understandings and a language for discussing them, but also primed the pump for new questions. ... Certainly, for this class, in the course of listening to each other call out their questions, the individual responsibility that they were willing to assume was clearly transformed into a collective sense of pleasure, the beginnings of commitment to this 'something' that we have created and are doing as a class, not something that is being imposed on us by a teacher. (Hume, 2001b)

At the beginning of the year in which the above episode occurred, Karen was surprised and dismayed when one student objected to the amount of time that was being spent on discussion; Andrew had wanted to get on with 'things that are really productive'. After considerable thought, Karen invited Andrew to carry out a collaborative inquiry with her on what made for more or less satisfactory class discussion. Several other students joined the group and, meeting regularly in the lunch hour, they discussed transcripts that Karen had prepared from video recordings of class discussions; then they even recorded and transcribed their own discussions. In order to capture the spirit and quality of this co-research, we will quote a passage from the chapter that Karen wrote about it.

> In coresearching the value of class discussions, my student colleagues and I have learned a great deal that will allow us to take action and become different. We have recognized the difficulty of tracking and maintaining conversations that encourage multiple points of entry and a wide variety of perspectives, while at the same time we've seen evidence of learning and stronger individual interest in the topic when we have such conversations ...
>
> When students become involved in knowledge building around action research issues they have the opportunity, likely for the first time, to experience the connections between knowledge and development, both individual and collective. I think this cannot help but change their

understanding of the nature of knowledge, helping them to recognize it as an object that can be continually improved through their active participation. When groups of students have this collaborative experience, the possibility exists for the creation of vital knowledge-building communities which may, through their example, transform the way we think about teaching, learning, and school. (Hume, 2001a)

Linking action, talk, and text

A third way of investigating the effect of adopting an inquiry orientation to the curriculum is to study one episode of whole-class discussion in considerable detail, set against the larger context of the curriculum unit in which it occurred. This reveals the relationship between individual moves and the development of 'public' or shared meanings that emerge over time, which then serve as resources for individual sensemaking. A close analysis of one episode is also an opportunity to foreground the intertextual links to other episodes that form the unit as a whole, and thus to describe more fully the relationship among 'learning', 'meaning' and 'understanding'.

The episode we have selected for analysis occurred during an exploratory curriculum unit that the classroom teacher designed in collaboration with the two authors. It took place in a fourth grade classroom in the central coast area of California; almost all the students spoke English fluently, although nearly half were of Mexican descent. The project was inspired by an event that the first author of this chapter had witnessed during an initial visit to the classroom – the annual 'Lunchbox Derby'. In preparation for this event, students had constructed vehicles out of fruit and vegetables, held together by wooden skewers. They were proud of their creations and anxious to win the competition to find out which vehicle could travel furthest across the carpet after rolling down an inclined wooden ramp. At the beginning of the next term, impressed by what he had seen, the first author approached Buzz, who agreed to treat the Lunchbox Derby as the 'launch' for a more extended investigation of how to make and improve vehicles to travel as far as possible from the bottom of the ramp. Several aims guided our approach:

- to involve the students in making decisions and plans for further activity;

- to engage them in developing understanding of the physics of motion while mastering the practical skills involved in the inquiry;

- to investigate whether and how this approach could promote exploratory talk in teacher/whole-class discussion.

In preparing for this second iteration, we made two important changes. The first was to assemble construction kits in order to supplement the materials students brought from home. This made it possible to spend less time on simple construction and more time on systematic tests of hypotheses about proposed modifications. The second change was to give each student an individual 'inquiry journal' in which they were instructed to record measurements and to document the modifications or conditions characterising different trial runs. As the project progressed, Buzz also asked the students to include predictions, to reflect on or explain their observations, and to summarise results.

The episode we focus on here is one of ten weekly sessions (of two hours each) that occurred midway through the second year of our collaborative intervention. On this occasion, the students were engaged in testing the effect of adding weight to their different car designs. This 'experiment' was not imposed; rather, it was largely the outcome of earlier discussions in which the teacher and some students had observed that the cars different groups had constructed had so many different features that it was difficult to decide why some went further than others. One of the most extreme and obvious differences between the different car designs was their weight, so it was not surprising that several students thought this was a variable worth systematic investigation.

For example, the results obtained showed that when one team added 25 pennies, their car travelled a shorter distance (275 inches) than it did without the added pennies (300 inches). Our expectation, on the other hand, based on our understanding of momentum (mass × velocity) was that (without complicating factors such as friction) additional weight would cause the cars to travel farther.

Such unexpected events are emblematic of authentic scientific inquiry and are key contributors to its progressive nature: results are produced that conflict with pre-existing theories or expectations and create the requirement for further investigation. Thus, when a teacher adopts an inquiry (as opposed to a more traditional) approach to curricular goals, such uncertainties lead to discussion and investigation rather than to passive acceptance of an authoritative conclusion. Accordingly, uncertain about what to make of the results, Buzz encouraged the students to produce their own interpretations of the results shown on the chart even as he continued to scaffold a joint focus of attention – as in this episode.

1: 13	**Buzz**	So, wh- what do you think about weight?
1: 14	**Bodey**	It doesn't help … it's worse.
1: 15	**Buzz**	It does work.
1: 16	**Sssss**	NO. [It doesn't help.] It's worse!
1: 17	**Buzz**	Oh it's WORSE I see. It doesn't help
1: 18	**Buzz**	Bodey?
1: 19	**Bodey**	Well I think it's the weight ... Like when it hits the flat on a – on a carpet … It like sorta like is a weight it's like it like umm … the um the ah chassis – we don't have one on ours – but all that connects (indicating plastic connector rods), the pennies is like pushing it DOWN so like the wheels kinda STOP and slow down – [Buzz: uhhuh] so it kinda, it goes umm not as <far>
1: 20	**Buzz**	Alright. So the weight coming down the ramp, pushing your car down, as soon as you hit the flat, it kind of pushes it DOWN, it's not pushing it down the ramp anymore, it pushes – it's weighting it down on the carpet so the wheels

On the one hand Buzz's second invitation, 'So what do you think about weight?' [line 1: 13], prioritises student contributions; on the other hand, it redirects student responses away from a simple comparison of distances travelled ('farther or not as far') and prompts comparisons relating distance to the presence or absence of added weight. Taking up this new two-dimensional comparison, Bodey, who is a relatively vocal student, interjects the suggestion [line 1: 14] that weight is 'worse' (meaning weight impedes cars from travelling as far as they would without weight, which several other students corroborate [line 1: 16]).

Bodey's following explanation [line 1 :18] is impressive not only because it considers how multiple factors interact (namely, how the weight affects the chassis, how this in turn might affect the function of the wheels on a carpet surface, and why that might slow the car down), but also because it draws attention to content that was not otherwise being considered *publicly* – namely, the performance of the wheels at the intersection of the ramp and the carpet.

By sidestepping Buzz's intended focus on understanding the relation-ship between added weight and distance, Bodey challenges/inspires other students to shift away from making merely descriptive contri-butions and to attempt explanations that answer 'why?' questions instead. This pivot is made possible because Buzz, an authority figure, not only accepts and revoices (O'Connor and Michaels, 1996) Bodey's proposal ('[added weight] pushes [the car] down … it's weighting it down on the carpet'), but also emphasises the potential this student's contribution has for understanding the recorded quantitative data.

On a later day, the class took the ramp outside and set it up to run the cars across the 'blacktop' asphalt. This proved to be a critical empirical move because outside on the asphalt they found that, contrary to the findings in the classroom, some cars did in fact travel farther when weight was added.

After that experiment the class went back inside and Buzz asked the students for their thoughts. This prompted one student, hardly able to stay in his seat, to excitedly volunteer his 'theory'.

> **Buzz:** Jerry, what do you think?
>
> **Jerry:** Well, er- . This is my theory of why weight helps when you're on the asphalt –
>
> **Buzz:** What do you mean, theory?
>
> **Jerry:** My theory like – . Well it's not really [inaudible] but it's like weight – why weight causes x the asphalt – . Cos the asphalt has little bumps which [inaudible] – the little bumps make the cars go UP a little bit and that slows them down. But with weight . Um it keeps the car um. Going to – going THROUGH the
>
> **Buzz:** That's a good theory …

Subsequently other students extended this theory, exploring and debating the effects of 'smooth' and 'bumpy' surfaces in relation to different kinds of wheels. The class also eventually decided to use a section of flexible poster board to extend the ramp and ease the 'impact' of the transition onto the floor to keep the cars from 'crashing'. This proved to be a pivotal modification, providing for more consistent and thus interpretable results.

We want to emphasise that none of these curricular developments was originally planned or anticipated by the teacher or visiting researchers. Instead, they can all be traced back and attributed to exploratory student contributions that emerged in the whole-class discussion format. However, this development did not come as a surprise, for it was exactly this kind of knowing and understanding through action and reflection that we had anticipated would emerge from the inquiry approach we had adopted.

In other words, the exploratory character of the dialogue observed in these whole-class discussions did not happen just by chance. Rather, it was the outcome of Buzz's commitment to a more comprehensive pedagogical approach in which students were expected to engage in some activity, reflect on that activity, and then decide what to do next. Thus, by being encouraged to introduce ideas that were truly generative for the inquiry as a whole, students gained a sense of agency or ownership in the learning process and became more committed to developing adequate explanations.

However, it is important not to underestimate Buzz's role as both manager and weaver. Indeed, this role requires a ceaseless balancing act between taking the lead from students and amplifying and interweaving their various contributions in furthering the curricular goals that he had in mind. On the one hand, productive opportunities to explore student perspectives can be missed if they are perceived as irrelevant or secondary instead of as potential sites of intertextual meaning making; on the other hand, in order for the conversations to be 'progressive' rather than disjointed and chaotic, Buzz had to remain active throughout the different conversations, redirecting different themes even as they were emerging, while still being willing to modify his own intended focus, on occasion, to allow and encourage the exploration of a student's potentially valuable contribution.

Conclusion

We began this chapter by explaining that we understand meaning, learning, and understanding as interactive processes that combine the ecological resources (both semiotic and material) available in a given situation and the joint efforts of individuals to communicate and engage in a collaborative action plan. Given this view, we assume that, in order for learners to appropriate meanings, they must be involved in the production of those meanings and their application to situations they see as relevant to their own activities and developing identities. In other words, in order for individuals to gain understanding they must become meaning makers and meaning users. We also assume here that cycles of meaning production, application and appropriation are impossible for individuals unless there is the real possibility of being understood and considered seriously by others. For these reasons we maintain that exploratory talk will be most productive when the following conditions apply.

- Individuals have opportunities to contribute opinions, suggestions, observations or experiences that they want to share and believe to be related to the activity in progress.

- Others are willing to listen attentively and critically.

- There are opportunities for all participants to discuss whether and in what ways different contributions are relevant.

- Experts share control and the right to evaluate with novices.

- The topic under discussion is, or becomes, of interest to the participants, where interest is most likely to be generated when the discussion bears on a future action to be carried out or on an 'object' that participants are constructing or trying to improve (for example, a model, performance, text, or explanation).

We would also maintain that students emerging from an experience in which they share in what has traditionally been the teacher's power to make decisions and set goals are more likely to believe their ideas and suggestions are important and so are also more likely to engage earnestly and publicly in classroom dialogue. In each of the examples presented in this chapter, classroom teachers were committed to a pedagogical model that prioritises student contributions and makes use of these contributions as points of departure for developing agendas. This is not to say, however, that the teachers do not also need to merge agendas or prioritise some agendas over others. Indeed, an important function of the teacher's role is to organise and manage selectively the available resources, including verbal contributions, in order to establish a coherent and productive joint focus of attention that can be shared and maintained by people with different perspectives yet which 'works' in relation to the situation and goals.

The teachers in each of the examples presented above found that an inquiry approach served as a way to generate truly collaborative objectives and action plans, and consequently to generate student engagement; at the same time, they also found that inquiry activities can function simultaneously, either to give focus to or constrain the range of options available for discussion. The selections from our research included in this chapter illustrate some of the conditions that follow from a commitment to inquiry as a pedagogical approach. Our discussion of the DICEP project foregrounds how discourse patterns shift away from an evaluative format to a more dialogic style when teachers endorse a collaborative approach to the curriculum and students have a sense that the questions they are investigating are important or consequential. The excerpt from Buzz's classroom inquiry into the physics of motion illustrates in detail how different interaction frames functionally constrain and afford the options available to speakers and interpreters of utterances in their co-construction of the content frames that mediate the development of shared meanings. All our examples illustrate that it is important for students to engage directly in collaborative activities that they can then draw on for discussion.

In this sense 'action' is a critical precondition for participation in exploratory talk, because discourse is not an end in itself but always serves some further purpose. People use language first and foremost to get things done, and to do them together. In this respect, an inquiry approach shifts the positional roles of students relative to teachers or other authority figures, allowing student contributions to become consequential for the meanings that develop. Students are more likely to integrate new (at least new to them) meanings into their own repertoires of practice if they have been active in their production and application.

Finally, it is worth reiterating a point that the first author of this chapter has previously articulated elsewhere (Wells, 1999; Wells and Mejía Arauz, 2006). In our view, adopting inquiry as a pedagogical approach means more than adopting piecemeal strategies such as increasing 'wait time' after a question, or including more 'hands-on' activities in the daily classroom repertoire. Adopting inquiry as a pedagogical approach means adopting a *dialogic stance* toward experiece and information, that is to say, a willingness on the part of all participants – teacher as well as students – to wonder, to ask questions and to attempt to answer those questions through the collection of relevant evidence by various means, both empirical and library-based, and to present the findings to one's peers for critical review and improvement. Most importantly, the ultimate aims of a dialogic stance are to foster in each student the lifelong dispositions to be agentive in learning and to collaborate with others in seeking for understanding that enables effective and responsible action.

References

Barnes, D. and Todd, F. (1977) *Communicating and Learning in Small Groups.* Abingdon: Routledge & Kegan Paul.

Brown, A.L., Ash, D. et al. (1993) 'Distributed expertise in the classroom', in G. Salomon (ed.), *Distributed Cognitions: Psychological and Educational Considerations.* Cambridge: Cambridge University Press.

Cazden, C. (1988) *Classroom Discourse: The Language of Teaching and Learning.* Portsmouth, NH: Heinemann.

Cole, M. (1996) *Cultural Psychology: A Once and Future Discipline.* Cambridge, MA: Bellknap.

Davis, G. (2001) 'A comparison of student-led discussions: class meetings and novel discussions', in G. Wells (ed.), *Talk, Text and Inquiry.* New York: Teachers College Press.

Dewey, J. (1938) *Experience and Education.* New York: Collier Macmillan.

Freire, P. (1970) *Pedagogy of the Oppressed.* New York: Herder and Herder.

Glassman, M. (2001) 'Dewey and Vygotsky: Society, experience, and inquiry in educational practice', *Educational Researcher*, 30 (4): 3–14.

Hume, K. (2001a) 'Seeing shades of grey: developing a knowledge building community', in G. Wells (ed.), *Talk, Text and Inquiry.* New York: Teachers College Press. pp. 99–117.

Hume, K. (2001b) 'Co-researching with students: exploring the value of class discussions', in G. Wells (ed.), *Talk, Text and Inquiry.* New York: Teachers College Press. pp.150–70.

Nassaji, H. and Wells, G. (2000) 'What's the use of triadic dialogue? An investigation of teacher–student interaction', *Applied Linguistics*, 21 (3): 333–63.

Nelson, K. (2007) *Young Minds in Social Worlds: Experience, Meaning and Memory.* Cambridge, MA: Harvard University Press.

O'Connor, M.C. and Michaels, S. (1996) 'Shifting participant frameworks: orchestrating thinking practices in group discussion', in D. Hicks (ed.), *Discourse, Learning, and Schooling.* New York: Cambridge University Press. pp. 63–103.

Scardamalia, M. and Bereiter, C. (1994) 'Computer Support for knoweldge–building communities. *Journal of the Learning Sciences*, 3(3): 265–83.

Tharp, R. and Gallimore, R. (1988) *Rousing Minds to Life.* New York: Cambridge University Press.

Vygotsky, L.S. (1987) 'Thinking and speech', in R.W. Rieber and A.S. Carton (eds), *The Collected Works of L.S. Vygotsky, Volume 1: Problems of General Psychology.* New York: Plenum. pp. 39–285.

Wells, G. (1986) *The Meaning Makers: Children Learning Language and Using Language to Learn.* Portsmouth, NH: Heinemann.

Wells, G. (1999) *Dialogic Inquiry: Towards a Sociocultural Practice and Theory of Education.* Cambridge: Cambridge University Press.

Wells, G. (ed.) (2001) *Action, Talk, and Text: Learning and Teaching Through Inquiry.* New York: Teachers College Press.

Wells, G. and Mejía Arauz, R. (2006) 'Dialogue in the classroom', *Journal of the Learning Sciences*, 15 (3): 379–428.

Note

1   Reports of these studies appeared in *Networks*, 6 (1) (2003). See http://journals. library.wisc. edu/titles/index.php/networks/issue/view/12

Index